T DE CONSTANTINOPLE

Solimanie

Palais de Constantin

St Dimitre

La Dar

Lavalidée

Pointe du Serail

Les Magasins de PERA

Le Serail

Tour de Leandre

DE THRACE

Tophana

CANAL DE LA MER NOI

e Serail de Scutari

Scutari

A POET'S BAZAAR

A POET'S BAZAAR

A JOURNEY TO GREECE, TURKEY & UP THE DANUBE

HANS CHRISTIAN ANDERSEN

Translated from the Danish & with an introduction by Grace Thornton

MICHAEL KESEND PUBLISHING · *New York*

Andersen's journey took him from Denmark through Europe to the Near East. The excerpts from his journals written in Germany and Italy come from Parts I and II of A *Poet's Bazaar*.

First American publication 1988
© Grace Thornton

Library of Congress Cataloging-in-Publication Data
Andersen, H. C. (Hans Christian), 1805–1875
   A poet's bazaar
   Translation of: En digters bazar.
   Includes index.
   1. Andersen, H. C. (Hans Christian), 1805–1875—
Journeys—Europe. 2. Andersen, H. C. (Hans Christian),
19th century—Journeys—Turkey. 3. Authors, Danish—
travel 1800–1918. 5. Turkey—Description and travel.
I. Title.
PT8118.A6   1987   389.8'18603 [B]   87-30993
ISBN 0-935576-23-1

Part One, *From Denmark to Malta* is printed with the permission of Peter Owen, Ltd.

Book design by Jacqueline Schuman

Manufactured in the United States of America

Endpapers: MUSEUM OF TURKISH AND ISLAMIC ARTS, ISTANBUL.

Frontispiece: *Hans Christian Andersen in a Fez*. Drawing by C. Hansen, 1841: PHOTO COLLECTION
GRACE THORNTON.

. . . the little bird chirruped, "It is lovely here in the North! It is good here in the North!" Nevertheless, the bird flew off to the warm lands, and the Poet did the same.

Contents

Part Four / JOURNEY UP THE DANUBE

Part Five / JOURNEY HOME

List of Illustrations

Introduction

"Come let us wander in imagination
Through the Bazaar, whose riches I present,
Its arching colonnades in panorama
From Copenhagen to the Orient."

This verse appeared on the title-page of the original edition of *En Digters Bazar (A Poet's Bazaar)*, the travel book which came out in 1842 of Hans Christian Andersen's long journey from Denmark to Turkey and the Black Sea—with an adventurous return up the Danube from Czernawoda to Vienna.

The journey, by steamer, carriage, and the newly constructed railroad would take the great story-teller almost nine months. His diary entries, beginning with his departure from Copenhagen on the last day of October, 1840, include vividly descriptive pictures of European and Middle Eastern life, original stories, fantasies and anecdotes—a rare portrait of another time and place.

At thirty-four, Andersen was already an established writer, in receipt of an annual State pension of 400 rigsdaler.[1] The poor shoemaker's son, who had arrived penniless in Copenhagen from Odense in 1819, had justified the faith shown in him by benefactors and friends during those hard early years. Socially he was now a regular, welcome and entertaining guest in family houses in Copenhagen and in castles and manors around the country. Professionally he was on his way to becoming well known abroad, particularly in Germany, as a poet and novelist, but he was still without the assured critical acclaim at home that was so essential for his peace of mind. "In Europe I am a *poet*, at home quite a decent person with a talent of a sort, but terribly vain. . . ." At the time of his departure for his *Bazaar* journey he was, as he said, sick at heart; his immediate reason for going was to escape

---

[1] A rigsdaler was equal to between 60¢ and $1.00 in U.S. currency.

from the critics—but, as always, restlessly he wanted to see something new. He had been earlier to Germany and Italy, but this time, health and money permitting, he hoped to get to Greece and even beyond.

In 1831, after severe criticism of his second volume of verse—he had been bitterly hurt at being described as "intoxicated by the ale of fantasy"[2] and because of the engagement and marriage to someone else of Riborg Voigt, with whom he had thought himself in love—he went to Germany and Switzerland. Out of this trip came his *Skygge-billeder* (Pictures of a Journey through the Hartz Mountains), a mixture of prose and poetry inspired by Heine's *Reisebilder*. It was reasonably well received.

In April 1833, with a travel grant from the Fondem ad Usos Publicos, of which his benefactor Jonas Collin was the Secretary, he went on a longer trip, through Germany, France and Switzerland to Italy, returning home (through Vienna and Prague) early in August 1834. Out of this there came, in April 1835, *Improvisatoren* (*The Improvisator*), a novel set in Rome and Capri. The book was a success both at home and abroad and was indeed the first work to make Andersen's name generally known in Europe. Between 1835 and 1851 it was translated into most of the European languages, including Russian and Czech.

On 8 May 1835, almost incidentally as it were, there appeared a small volume of four stories for children: *The Tinder Box, Little Claus and Big Claus, The Princess on the Pea* and *Little Ida's Flowers*.

In a letter of March 1835 to his dear friend Henrietta Wulff, he had said that he had recently written a novel, a play and some tales for children "about which Ørsted says that if *The Improvisator* will make me famous, these will make me immortal, they are the most perfect things I have written. But I don't believe that at all. . . ." And for a long time he really did not believe it although, perhaps significantly, the title-page had said "Volume I."[3]

---

[2] Henrik Hertz, *Letters from a Ghost* (December 1830).
[3] Volume II appeared in December 1835, and Volume III in April 1837 (including *The Little Mermaid* and *The Emperor's New Clothes*). Further selections continued annually. *The Ugly Duckling* came in 1843. The first English translation was in 1846.

He continued to write poems and novels: *O.T.* in April 1836 and *Kun en Spillemand* (*Only a Fiddler*) in November 1837, both as usual autobiographical, and both were successful and soon translated. His short, usually one-act, plays were mostly successful, but Andersen's real ambition was to achieve fame as a serious dramatic writer.

His *Agnete and the Merman* had to be printed privately, since no publisher could be found to take it. News of this rebuff reached Andersen in January 1834 in a letter from Edvard Collin, which reduced him to bitter despair. (When the play was eventually produced at the Royal Theatre in April 1843, it was booed.)

Andersen's next play, "*The Mulatto*," was his biggest serious dramatic success so far. In the same year he wrote another play, *Maurerpigen* (*The Moorish Girl*), which was at once accepted by the Royal Theatre and its première scheduled for 18 December 1840. But there were serious production difficulties. He had written the leading part, Raphaella, for the actress wife of Johann Ludvig Heiberg, the then arbiter of dramatic taste in Copenhagen and one of Andersen's severest critics. The Heibergs turned the play down. Another actress was found and production went ahead, but Andersen was furious and, sad to say, not only abused the Heibergs to all his friends but allowed himself to write an obviously self-pitying preface to the play, which was further fuel for the critics' fire.

He decided not to wait for the première but to take another long journey abroad, and he left Denmark on 31 October 1840. The Collins must have been relieved to see him go. The youngest of the family, Louise, was about to be married. Andersen had, some years before, fancied himself in love with her and he would surely have been a gloomy guest at the wedding of his "lost rose." So off he went and, almost in spite of himself, found much to enjoy and, with his keen eye, much to record.

He enjoyed his German experiences, including hearing Franz Liszt in concert, and taking his first ride on the newly built railway. Italy was, however, disappointing and not the smiling land of magic memories from his time there in 1833–4. The weather was bad with storms and earth tremors, and the Tiber was in flood. He had his usual toothache and a bad throat, and in the background were worries about money and the fate of *The Moorish Girl*. On New Year's day he went to St. Peter's and prayed, "Oh God, give me an immortal name as a writer, give me health and give me peace."

At last, nearly a month after the 18 December première, he heard that the reception of *The Moorish Girl* had been unenthusiastic and that the play had been taken off after only three nights. It was a financial disaster. Once again it was a letter from Edvard Collin that really hurt him. Edvard had written: "If you think the unfavorable criticism of *The Moorish Girl* has left any lasting impression in your disfavor, you are mistaken, for it is already forgotten." ". . . . for another significant literary *Erscheinung* has now taken its place—namely Heiberg's *New Poems*, of their kind and in their excellent form a most remarkable product."[4]

This failure was as bad as if not worse than that of *Agnete and the Merman* which wrecked his New Year in Rome in 1834. Andersen was convinced that he was facing literary and financial extinction and he wanted to die.

He went on to Naples at the beginning of March and there he was truly ill and had to be bled. He had given up all hope of going on to Greece when suddenly he heard that King Christian had given him a travel grant of 600 rigsdaler to enable him to continue his journey.

For those of Andersen's generation with a classical education, Greece seemed to be known ground, with its mythology, legend, art and ancient history all part of Western culture. But, in plain fact, most of what he and others actually saw was sadly unfamiliar: there was no trace of the god-like figures of classical sculpture; above ground, only ruins and heaped stones offered any impression of the glory that was once Greece. After centuries of subjugation by the Turks, the Greeks

---

[4] The literary sequel to Andersen's ill-fated play was Heiberg's *A Soul After Death*. It was a satire in which the damned were condemned to sit through performances of *The Mulatto* and *The Moorish Girl*—Hell being not a place of fire and brimstone but a "repetition ad infinitum of the soulless existence he (the lost soul) had always been living" (Bredsdorff, p. 148). H.C.A. settled this particular account by portraying in his description of quarantine on the journey up the Danube (see p. 165), an Heibergian *Inferno* with a generous tribute to Heiberg's latest work in a footnote.

had at last rebelled in 1821, with temporary success. Western opinion was aroused partly as a result of Byron's expedition and his death in Missolonghi in December 1824. In the decisive Battle of Navarino in October 1827 the British, French and Russians destroyed the combined Turkish and Egyptian fleets; the Treaty of Adrianople in 1830 declared Greece an independent kingdom.

After the assassination of their first President, Capodistrias in 1831, Prince Otto of Bavaria was chosen to be King. It was this young man and his German-born wife, Amalie, that Andersen met in Athens and much admired—realizing the overwhelming task of national reconstruction that faced them and their Government.

For travel in Turkey there was no equivalent to the classical education for the student of Greece. Andersen had read Lamartine's *Souvenirs d'un voyage en Orient 1835*, in a Danish translation, and on board the *Lycurgus*, from Syra to the Piraeus, he had borrowed Eugène Boré's *Correspondance et mémoires d'un voyageur en Orient*. But, as he said in his Journal, fantasy was what was needed for travel in the Orient, and this he had in plenty.

In 1841, Turkey was still recovering from the traumas of the previous two decades—the loss of Greece and the running dispute with Mehemet Ali in Egypt. In Europe, the control of the Ottoman Empire extended as far as Moldavia and Wallachia (now both Rumania), Bulgaria and Serbia (now Yugoslavia). The young Sultan, Abdul Mesched, was to do his best in initiating reforms, not least as regards the status of his Christian subjects. But an inevitable tide of insurrection and nationalism was not to be stemmed forever.

From Constantinople Andersen could return home either the way he had come, through Greece and Italy, or he could go up to the Black Sea and from there make his way up the Danube to Vienna and thence to Denmark.

Before the introduction of steam navigation in 1830 it had not been possible to sail up the Danube; until then the force of the currents and natural hazards like the Iron Gate had limited the use of the river to downstream traffic. But, ten years later, the sailing upstream was not exactly smooth.

When he went abroad, Andersen invariably sought out the company of his fellow countrymen, diplomats, artists, writers and others with whom he could talk and feel at ease—and accepted. This did not, however, mean that he was oblivious to the "native" life around him for, with all his imagination, he was a realist. Again and again in his stories he made a valid social statement—often very biting—and in his travel books the people in the landscape are by no means just lay figures: they have a life of their own, acutely observed—from the Turkish child with the toy on board the steamer in the Sea of Marmora to the sad but proud little Hungarian boy who wanted to be an Officer.

But Hans Christian Andersen was not a political animal, not a political journalist—he was a poet, with a genius for communicating in prose his own visual experience.

Once again, I can but hope that I have done him justice.

Grace Thornton

Part One

FROM
DENMARK
TO MALTA

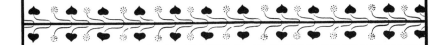

Liszt

It was in Hamburg, in the hotel Stadt London, that Liszt was giving a concert. The hall was absolutely full in a very few minutes. I arrived late, but nevertheless got the best place near the platform. I was taken up the back stairs. Liszt is one of the kings in the kingdom of music and my friends, as I said, took me to him up the back stairs—I am not ashamed to admit it.

The hall, even the side-rooms, shone with lights, gold necklaces and diamonds. Not far from where I stood, a fat and painted Jewess lady lay on a sofa; she looked like a walrus with a fan. Solid Hamburg merchants stood close-packed beside each other, as if some important exchange affair were to be negotiated. A smile played round their lips, as though they had all bought shares and made a fortune. With his playing, the mythological Orpheus could move stones and trees—the new Orpheus, Liszt, had electrified this audience even before he played. Rumor, reputation with its mighty "nimbus," had opened folks' eyes and ears, so that they all seemed to recognize in advance what was to follow. I felt this expectation myself. In the musical world our generation has two princes of the piano, Thalberg and Liszt.

It was as if an electric current went through the hall when Liszt entered. Most of the ladies rose, and each face lit up as if seeing a dearly loved friend. I stood quite near to the artist; he is a thin, pale young man with long, dark hair. He bowed and sat down at the piano. The first impression I had of his personality was the expression of great passion in his wan face. He seemed to me a demon, nailed fast to the instrument from which music poured out—the notes came from his blood, from his thoughts. He was a demon who had to play to liberate his soul, he was on the rack, the blood flowed and the nerves trembled. But as he played, so the demonic disappeared. I saw the pale face take on a more noble and more beautiful expression; the divine soul shone

3

from his eyes and out of every feature—he was handsome, transformed by spirit and passion.

His *Valse Infernale* is more than a daguerreotype picture of Meyerbeer's *Robert*. We do not stand outside and look at a well-known painting—no, we are taken right inside, we stare down into the very abyss and see new whirling figures. It did not sound like the powerful tones of a pianoforte; every note seemed like a cascade of water.

One often uses the expression "a sea of music" without explanation, and it is this that streams out of the piano. The instrument seems to be transformed into a whole orchestra. It all comes from ten fingers that have a skill which can only be called fanatical—the fingers of a great genius.

I have met politicians who, under the influence of Liszt's playing, understood how the peaceful citizen could be so gripped by the sound of the *Marseillaise* as to seize his rifle, leave hearth and home and fight for an idea. With his playing I have seen peaceful Copenhageners—with Danish autumn mists in their blood—become political Bacchants. The traveler—I end with myself—finds tone-pictures of what he is seeing or will see: I heard his playing like an overture to my journey. I heard my heart beating and bleeding at leaving home. I heard the waves saying "farewell," the waves that I should not hear again until I reached the cliffs of Terracina. It sounded like the organ notes from Germany's old cathedrals, avalanches rolled from the Alps and Italy danced in carnival dress, while it remembered in its heart Caesar, Horace and Raphael. Vesuvius and Etna erupted, the oracle spoke from the mountains of Greece where the gods are dead, and tones I did not recognize, tones I have no words for, spoke of the Orient, the land of fantasy, the poet's second fatherland.

When Liszt had finished playing, flowers rained down all round him. Pretty young women, old ladies who had once been pretty young women, each threw her bouquet. He had cast a thousand bouquets of melody into their hearts and heads.

From Hamburg Liszt was going to London, there to scatter new musical flowers, to touch with poetry its material, everyday life. Fortunate man who can so journey all his life, always seeing people in their spiritual Sunday best—yes, even in the bridal dress of wonder!

Would I meet him again was my last thought. And chance had it that we should meet on this journey, meet in a place where I and my reader would least expect it—meet, become friends and part again. But that belongs to the last chapter.

The Railway

Since many of my readers have never seen a railway, I shall try first of all to give an impression of one. Let us take an ordinary public highway: it can go straight on or round a bend, to left or right, but it must be level, level as a drawing-room floor, and for this reason we tunnel every mountain that gets in the way, and over marsh and deep valleys we build bridges on strong arches. When the level road is finished, where the tracks will run we lay iron rails on it, on which the wagon-wheels can take hold. The steam-engine is made fast at the front with the driver in charge who know how to steer and to stop it. Wagon is linked to wagon, filled with people or cattle—and off we go.

The precise time of the train's arrival there is known at each station on the way: for miles around too one can hear the whistle of the signal when the train is in motion and, where side-roads for ordinary traffic and pedestrians cross the railway, the waiting guard lets down a wooden barrier across the road and the good folk must wait until we have passed. All along the track from one end to the other, small houses are built with such a distance between that the guards who live there can see each other's flags and make certain in good time that their part of the track is clear of stones and branches.

So there is a railway, and I hope my readers have understood!

It was the first time in my life that I was to see one. From Braunschweig to Magdeburg it was half a day and a night by diligence—the roads were very bad and I was tired when we reached Magdeburg. I was to leave again by train an hour later. I cannot deny that I had, in anticipation, a feeling that I can only call railway-fever and it was at its heights when I entered the splendid building from which the trains depart. There was a throng of travelers, people rushing about with baggage and carpet-bags, engines whistling and snorting as they puffed out steam. On the first occasion the traveler does not really know where he dare stand so as not to find himself under a carriage, a steam-boiler or a load of freight; but in fact one stands safe and sound on a platform and the carriages for the passengers are drawn right up alongside in a row, like gondolas by a quay. But outside the station the iron rails cross like magic ribbons, one after another, and it is in fact a magic chain that human wisdom has forged. Our magic coaches must keep within it—if they come outside the magic chain there is danger to life and limb. I gazed at these locomotives, the loose wagons, the moving chimneys and God knows what, which all seemed to be jumbled together in a magic world. Everything seemed to be moving. And now the steam and the noise, in conjunction with the crowding to get seats, the smell of tallow, the regular pulsing of the engines, the whistle and snort of escaping steam, all this heightened the impression. And if one is there, as I was, for the first time, one expects to be knocked down, to break an arm or leg, to be thrown into the air or crushed between two rows of carriages. But I fancy it is only on the first occasion that one thinks of all this.

The train here had three sections. The first two were commodious, closed carriages, just like our diligences but much broader. The third consisted of open compartments that even the poorest peasant could afford to use because they were so cheap—it was less dear than a long journey by road, with stops for refreshment and perhaps overnight at inns on the way. The signal is given, but it is not an attractive noise— it sounds rather like a pig's "swan song" when the knife pierces its neck. One sits in the commodious carriage, the conductor locks the door and takes the key, but we can let down the window and enjoy the fresh air without any fear of draughts. It is really like being in any other sort of carriage, only more comfortable—one can relax, when one has had an exhausting journey only a short time before.

The first sensation one has is a very gentle jerk in the carriages as the chains which hold them together are stretched taut. The whistle sounds again and we are off, but slowly—the first steps are gentle, like a child's hand pulling a little carriage. The train gathers speed, but imperceptibly; you read your book or look at a map and are not

A steam train of Andersen's time is crowded with passengers both inside and out. "What a tremendous effect this invention has on the spirit," wrote Andersen. "One feels so powerful, just like a magician of olden days."

really sure that the journey has properly begun, because the coach glides like a sledge on a smooth snowfield. You look out of the window and realize that you are racing away like a horse at the gallop. The speed increases, you appear to be flying, but there is no shaking, no draught, nothing at all unpleasant as you had expected! What was that red thing that went like a streak of lightning close by? It was one of the guards, standing with his flag. Just look out! The nearest fields go by in an arrow-swift stream, grass and plants run into each other— one has the feeling of standing outside the globe and watching it turn. It hurts one's eyes to look for too long in the same direction; but if you look somewhat farther away, other things do not move any quicker

than we see them move when we are driving at a good pace, and farther out on the horizon everything seems to stand still—one has a view and impression of the whole district.

This is precisely how one should travel through flat country. It is as though towns lie close together, now one, now another! This is how towns must appear to birds of passage in flight. The ordinary travelers on the by-roads seem to be stationary. Horses in front of carts lift their feet but seem to put them down again in the same place—and so we have gone by them.

There is a well-known anecdote about an American who was on a train for the first time and saw one milestone after another rushing by in a continuous stream, and he thought he was driving through a cemetery and was seeing monuments. I should not really quote this, but it does give a good picture of speed and I remembered this story—although there were no milestones, there were red signal-flags instead, and the same American could have said here, why is everyone out today with red flags!

On the other hand, I shall tell a story against myself. As we went by a fence that I saw foreshortened to one plank, a man beside me said, "We are now in the Principality of Cöthen," took a pinch of snuff and offered me the box. I bowed, took a pinch, sneezed and said, "How long shall we be in Cöthen?" "Oh," answered the man, "we left it while you were sneezing."

And yet steam-engines can go twice as fast as we were going then. Every few minutes we stop at a station, with passengers to be set down and others taken on, and the speed therefore is reduced. When we stop for a moment, through the open windows waiters offer us refreshments, light or solid as we wish. Against payment, roast pigeons fly literally into the mouth and so we are away again. We read or look at Nature and see how often a herd of cows turns around, astonished, or some horses break loose and flee when they see that twenty wagons can get on in the world without them—and more speedily than with their help. And so we are suddenly again under a roof, where the train stops—we have traveled over sixty miles in three hours and are in Leipzig. The same day, four hours later, another train goes a similiar distance in the same time, but through mountains and over rivers to Dresden.

I have heard many say that the coming of the railway would be the end of the poetry and romance of travel and that everything beautiful and interesting would be lost. So far as interest is concerned, everyone is free to go to any station he likes and there to look around him until the next train arrives. And as for the disappearance of the poetry of travel, I am of the completely opposite opinion. It is in the cramped, overfilled stage-coaches and diligences that poetry vanishes. In them one becomes dull, and in the best of weather one is plagued by dust and heat and in the winter by bad roads. One does not enjoy the countryside in greater portions, only in longer hauls than in a train.

And what a tremendous effect this invention has on the spirit! One feels so powerful, just like a magician of olden days. We harness the magic horse to our carriage and space disappears. We fly like clouds before the storm, as birds of passage fly. Our wild horse sniffs and snorts, black steam rising from his nostrils. Mephistopheles could not fly more quickly with Faust in his cloak. By natural means we are, in our day, as powerful as in the Middle Ages man thought only the devil could be. With our wisdom we have drawn alongside him—and before he knows it, we have passed him by.

I remember but few times in my life when I have felt myself so affected as here, as though with all my mind and being I was face to face with God. I felt a devotion such as I have felt only as a child in church and, as an adult, in a sunlit wood or on a dead-calm sea on a star-clear night. In the kingdom of Poetry, feeling and fantasy are not the only rulers—they have a brother who is just as powerful. His name is Understandiing, he proclaims the eternal truth, and therein lie greatness and poetry.

December 4–5, 1840, in the Appenines

. . . I rested my forehead against the iron bars of my window and felt myself no more alone than I am in my little room in Denmark. He who has a proper home can feel homesick; he who has no home feels himself equally at home everywhere. After a few minutes my room here had become home for me, although I did not yet know the surroundings . . .

and over the Brenner Pass into Italy

. . . The road went down, picturesque and lovely, snaking around in serpentine twists and turns, then through walled arches, always in the shelter of the hills, where the sun shone warm, where the snow had melted and the trees were in leaf. "Lovely Italy!" we all rejoiced, and the coachman cracked his whip and Echo sent back the sound.

The Bronze Boar (A STORY)

In the city of Florence, not far from the Piazza del Granduca, there is a little side-street, I think it is called Porta Rossa, and there in front of a kind of market where they sell vegetables is a very attractive, well-cast bronze boar. Fresh, clear water spouts from the mouth of the animal, which is dark green with age: only the snout shines as though polished—and so it is, daily by hundreds of children and beggars, who cup their hands round it and put their mouths to that of the boar to drink. It is a picture to see this beautifully made animal embraced by a handsome, half-naked boy, his fresh young mouth against its snout.

Everyone who comes to Florence can easily find the place. He has only to ask the first beggar he meets about the bronze boar, and he will find it.

It was a late winter evening: the snow lay on the mountains, but there was a moon, and moonlight in Italy gives a light which is just as bright as a dark winter day in the North—in fact brighter, because the air is clear and it seems to invigorate, while in the North a cold, gray, lead-gray roof seems to press us down to the earth, the cold, damp earth which will, in the end, press down on our coffins.

In the gardens of the Duke's palace, where thousands of roses bloom in winter, under the shelter of a pine tree a ragged little boy had sat all day, a boy who could have sat as a model for Italy—beautiful, laughing and, at the same time, suffering. He was hungry and thirsty: no one had given him any money, and when it grew dark and the garden was to be closed, the gatekeeper drove him out. He stood for a long time on the bridge over the Arno, dreaming and looking at the reflections shimmering in the water of the twinkling stars, of the magnificent marble bridge, Della Trinità, and his own image between them. He made his way to the bronze boar, crouched down and, putting his arms around its neck, put his little mouth to its gleaming snout and drank the fresh water in great gulps. Close by lay some lettuce-leaves and a few chestnuts. These were his supper. There was not a single person in the street, he was quite alone. He climbed up on to the animal's back, leaned forward so that his curly head rested on that of the boar and, before he knew it, he was fast asleep.

It was midnight. The bronze boar moved and the child heard it say, quite distinctly, "Little boy, hold on tight, for I am now going to run." And run it did, and it was the oddest ride imaginable. First they came to the Piazza del Granduca, and the bronze horse bearing the statue of the Duke neighed loudly. The colored crests on the old town hall shone like transparent pictures and Michelangelo's David swung his sling. There was movement and life everywhere. The figures around the statue of Perseus and on that of the *Rape of the Sabine Women* were too much alive—the death cries of the women echoed over the magnificent, deserted square.

By the Palazzo degli Uffizi, in the arcade where the nobility gather for Carnival, the bronze boar stopped. "Hold tight," it said, "hold tight, because now I am going up the stairs."

The child said not a word; he was half-afraid, half-happy.

They went into a long gallery, which he knew well, because he had been there before. The walls were adorned with pictures, with statues and busts all around. There was a wonderful light everywhere, as if it were day, but the most wonderful moment was when the door to one of the side-rooms opened—and this the boy would always remember: everything that night was at its most beautiful. Here stood a lovely, naked woman, as beautiful as only Nature and the greatest master in marble could make her. She moved her lovely limbs, dolphins leaped by her feet, immortality shone out of her eyes. The world calls her the Venus dei Medici. On each side were marble statues and sculptures in which the life of the spirit had permeated the stone. There were handsome naked men: one was grinding a sword, wrestling gladiators made up another group—the sword was sharpened and the men fought for the Goddess of Beauty.

The boy was almost blinded by the radiance. The very walls shone with color. But none of the pictures dared to leave their frames. Even the Goddess of Beauty, the gladiators and the sword-grinder stayed on their pedestals, perhaps constrained by the golden light of the haloes of the Madonna, Jesus and John. These holy pictures were no longer just pictures—they were the Holy Ones themselves.

What beauty, what loveliness there was in every room. The child saw it all, for the bronze boar went step by step through the gallery. But one picture above all caught his imagination and stayed with him, chiefly because of the happy, carefree children in it, children to whom he had once in daylight nodded a greeting. Many people probably pass quickly by this picture, and yet it contains a wealth of poetry. It is of Christ, descending into the Underworld—but it is not the damned one sees around him, no, it is the heathen. The painter is Angelo Bronzino, a Florentine. Most moving is the expression on the faces of the children—an expression of certainty that they will go to Heaven. Two small children already embrace each other, one stretches out his hand to another below and points at himself as if to say, "I am going to Heaven!" All the older people stand uncertain, hoping, or they kneel humbly, praying to the Lord Jesus.

The boy looked longer at this picture than at any other. The bronze boar rested quietly in front of it: a gentle sigh was heard—did it come from the picture or from the animal? The boy lifted his hand towards the smiling children, and at that moment the animal moved off with him, away through the open entrance hall.

"Thank you and God bless you, you wonderful creature!" said the little boy and patted the bronze boar which, bumpity-bump, went down the steps with him on his back.

"Thank you and God bless you," said the bronze boar. "I have helped you and you have helped me, for only when an innocent child is on my back do I have the power to run! Yes, I dare even stand under the rays of the lamp in front of the picture of the Madonna. I can take you everywhere—only not into the church! But with you on my back I can stand outside and look in through the open door. Do not get down, for if you do I shall be dead, as dead as I am when you see me in daytime in the Porta Rossa."

"I will stay with you, my blessed animal," said the child, and so they went whizzing through the streets of Florence, on to the square in front of the Church of Santa Croce. The great doors sprang open, light streamed from the altar, through the church and out on to the deserted square. In the left aisle an other-worldly radiance came from a monument around which a thousand twinkling stars seemed to form a halo. A coat of arms decorated the stone—on a blue ground, a scarlet ladder which glowed like flame. It was the grave of Galileo, a simple monument, but the red ladder on the blue ground is a significant crest: it could be that of Art itself, for the way of Art is always upwards—up a ladder of fire—but it reaches to Heaven. All the Prophets of the Spirit ascend to Heaven as did the Prophet Elijah. In the right aisle all the figures on the rich sarcophagi seemed to be alive. Here stood Michelangelo, there Dante with the laurel wreath on his brow. Alfieri, Machiavelli—side by side rest these great men, the pride of Italy.[1] It is a beautiful church, far more lovely though not so large as the cathedral of Florence.

The marble clothes seemed to move as the great figures appeared to turn their heads, to look out into the night. There was music and singing, and by the gleaming altar white-clad boys swung gilded censers, from which the pungent smell of incense filled the air, drifting through the church and out to the open square.

The boy stretched out his arms towards the light, and at that moment the bronze boar turned and ran away so quickly that he had to hold on tight. The wind whistled in his ears and he heard the church door rattle on its hinges and it shut fast. He seemed to lose consciousness and felt a biting cold—and then he opened his eyes.

It was morning. He was sitting, half-fallen off the bronze boar, which stood where it always stood, in the Porta Rossa. The child thought of the woman he called Mother and was very frightened. She had sent him out yesterday, telling him to beg for money—he had

---

[1] Opposite Galileo's grave is that of Michelangelo: on the monument is his bust and three figures, representing sculpture, painting and architecture. Close by is Dante's monument—his body is in Ravenna. On this monument Italy is pointing towards the colossal statue of Dante, while Poetry weeps for the Lost One. A few steps away is the memorial to Alfieri, decorated with laurel-leaves, lyres and masks: Italy is weeping over his tomb. Machiavelli is the last in this line of famous men.

collected none and was hungry and thirsty. Once again he put his arms round the boar's head, kissed it on the snout, nodded goodbye and made his way home to a narrow alley, just broad enough for a laden donkey to pass. A heavy, iron-studded door stood ajar. He went through it and up a stone stairway with filthy walls and a frayed rope for a banister. Above there was an open gallery hung around with ragged clothing. Another stairway led down to the courtyard with a well in the middle, from which heavy wires were strung across to each story of the house. On these, buckets wobbled up and down, while the pulley whistled and the pails danced in the sun, water splashing down into the yard.

The boy went up another decaying stone stairway. Two cheerful Russian sailors, returning from their nightly Bacchanal, charged down the stairs and nearly knocked the wretched child down. A woman, not young but with a full figure and thick dark hair, was standing behind them. "How much have you got?" she said to the boy.

"Don't be cross," he begged. "I got nothing, nothing at all," and he grabbed the hem of her skirt as though to kiss it.

They went into the room, which I really cannot bring myself to describe. Suffice it to say that there was a pot filled with charcoal—they call it *marito*. The woman put her hands round it to warm her fingers, then poked the boy with her elbow, screaming, "Of course you've got money!"

The child burst into tears. She kicked him with her foot and he howled the louder. "Be quiet or I'll break your bawling head!" She swung the pot she was holding in her hands and the boy ducked down with a scream.

This brought in the woman from next door. She too was holding her *marito* under her arm. "Felicita! What are you doing to the child?"

"He's my child," retorted Felicita. "I can murder him if I want to—and you as well, Gianina!" And she swung her pot of charcoal in the air.

The other woman raised hers to ward off the blow and the two jars cracked together—potsherds and burning charcoal and ashes flew around the room.

But the boy had fled, out of the door, across the yard and out of the tenement. The poor child ran until he could no longer draw breath and stopped by the Church of Santa Croce, the church whose great doors had opened up for him last night, and he went inside. The lights were on and he knelt down by the first monument on the right, Michelangelo's, and sobbed his heart out. People came and went, Mass was said, and no one took any notice of the child, save one elderly man who stopped, looked at him and then went on his way like all the others. The boy was wracked with hunger and thirst and felt weak and ill. He huddled down between the wall and the monument and fell asleep.

It was getting on towards evening when he was awakened by someone shaking him. He got up and saw the same elderly man standing in front of him. "Are you ill? Where do you live? Have you been here all day?" The man poured out his questions, which the child answered and then they went off together to a little house in one of the side-streets nearby.

It was a glove-maker's workshop. They went in and found the wife sitting and sewing industriously. A small white poodle, so close-clipped that one could see its pink skin, jumped on to the table and welcomed the boy. "Innocent souls recognize each other," said the woman, patting both dog and child.

The good couple gave him something to eat and drink and said he should spend the night there. The next day, Papa Giuseppe would go and talk to his mother. The boy was given a little bed—it was poor enough, but royal luxury to one who had so often had to sleep on the cold stone floor. He slept soundly and dreamed about the wonderful pictures and the bronze boar.

Papa Giuseppe went out the next morning and the child was very worried, because he was sure that he would have to go back to his mother. He cried and kissed the lively little dog, and the good wife nodded to them both.

But Papa Giuseppe came back home with other news. He talked a long time with his wife, who nodded her head and patted the child. "He is a nice little boy," she said. "He can become as good a glove-maker as you are—look at his fingers, how slender and flexible they are. Our Lady has intended him for a glove-maker!"

And so the boy stayed on in the house and the woman taught him to sew. He ate well and slept well: he became mischievous and began to tease Bellissima, the little dog. This made the woman very angry and she shook her fist at him and scolded him roundly. The boy took this to heart and went and sat, very thoughtful, in his little room. This room looked out on to the street and the dried skins were stored there, so there were thick iron bars over the windows. He could not sleep: he was thinking of the bronze boar—and, suddenly, he heard a noise outside—clippety-clop—surely that was the boar! He sprang to the window, but there was nothing to be seen, the street was empty.

"Help the Signor to carry his paintbox," said the woman the next morning to the boy. This was the young neighbor, a painter, who was trying with difficulty to carry both his paints and a heavy rolled canvas. The child took the box and followed the artist—and they went off to the gallery and mounted the same staircase that he knew well from the night he had ridden there on the bronze boar. He recognized the statues and the pictures, the lovely marble Venus and the living, painted figures. He saw again the Mother of God, Jesus and John. Now they stopped before the Bronzino picture, in which Christ goes down to the Underworld and the children round Him smile, in their sweet foretaste of Heaven. The poor little boy smiled too, for here he was in his Heaven!

"Now, off home with you," said the painter, when he saw that the boy was still there after he had set up his easel.

"Can't I watch you paint?" said the child. "Can't I see how you make a picture appear on the canvas?"

"I am not going to paint yet," said the artist, and taking his black crayon he moved his hand quickly across the canvas, measuring the great picture with his eye—and there was the figure of Christ, faint but clear, as on the painting. "And now, go!" said the man, and the boy went quietly home, sat up on the table—and learned to sew gloves.

But for the rest of the day his thoughts were in the picture gallery and he pricked his fingers, was clumsy, and did not once tease Bellissima! When it was evening he noticed that the door was ajar and he crept out. It was a beautiful starlit night but cold, and he walked slowly through the already silent streets. Soon he was standing in front of the bronze boar. He bent down, kissed its polished snout and then sat himself on its back. "You blessed creature," he said. "I have missed you so much! Tonight we must go for a ride."

But the bronze boar stood motionless, the fresh water spurting from its mouth. The child sat astride like a rider. Suddenly he felt something tugging at his ankles—he looked down and there was Bellissima, the little clipped dog. It had followed the boy out of the house without his noticing and was now barking as if to say, "Look—here I am and why are you sitting up there?"

A fiery dragon could not have frightened the child more than did the appearance of the dog—here was Bellissima out in the street and without being dressed, as the woman called it! What would happen? The dog was never allowed out in winter without the little sheepskin coat that had been specially made for it: the skin was fastened with a red band round the neck, belted under the stomach and decorated with ribbons and bells. The dog looked almost like a little lamb when it was thus dressed up in winter and allowed to trip out with its mistress. What *would* happen? All his dreams vanished, but the boy kissed the bronze boar as he picked up Bellissima, who was shivering with cold, and ran as fast as he could towards home.

"What are you running away with there?" called two gendarmes whom he met, and Bellissima began to howl. "Where did you steal this beautiful dog?" they demanded and took it from him.

"Oh, please give it back to me!" wailed the boy.

"If you haven't stolen it, you can tell them at home that they can collect it at the guard-post." And they gave him the address and went off with the dog.

He was in despair. He did not know whether to jump into the Arno or to go home and confess. They would surely kill him, he thought. "But I should like to be killed! If I did, I shall go to Jesus and Our Lady!" And he went home, hoping to be killed.

The door was closed and he could not reach the knocker: there was no one about in the street, but he found a stone and hammered on the door with it.

"Who's there?" they called from inside.

"It's me," he said. "Bellissima has got out. Let me in—and then kill me!"

There was a great to-do, especially on the part of the wife, about the wretched Bellissima. She saw at once that the little sheepskin coat was still hanging on its peg on the wall. "Bellissima at the guard-post!" she screamed. "You wicked child, why did you take her out? She'll freeze to death! Think of that fine, delicate creature with those ruffians of soldiers."

The husband had to go off at once, while the woman screamed and the boy wept. All the neighbors came in, including the artist, who took the boy on his knee and asked him what had happened. Little by little he got the whole story, about the bronze boar and the gallery. It was not easy to understand. The artist comforted the child and tried to calm the woman, but she was not to be reassured until her husband came back with Bellissima. Everyone was happy then and the artist patted the wretched child on the head and gave him some pictures. They were wonderful—and some were comical! But one above all he loved—one of the bronze boar itself and absolutely lifelike: only a few strokes on paper and there it was, and even the house behind was there too. If you can draw and paint, you can call the whole world your own, he thought.

The next day, as soon as he had a moment to himself, the boy grabbed a crayon and on the back of one of the pictures he tried to copy the drawing of the bronze boar—and it worked. It was, admittedly, a little crooked—a bit up and down, one leg thick, another thin—but it was recognizable and he was jubilant! The crayon would not move as smoothly as it should, this he could well see, but the next day there was a second bronze boar beside the first and it was a hundred times better. The third was so good that anyone could have recognized it.

But the glove-making went badly and errands in the city took longer and longer, for the bronze boar had taught him that every picture could be put on paper, and the city of Florence is a whole picture-book for everyone who cares to turn the pages. On the Piazza della Trinità there stands a slender column, on the top of which there is the Goddess of Justice, blindfolded and with scales in her hand. She was soon on paper, and it was the glove-maker's little boy who had put her there. The picture collection was growing, but all the pictures were of dead things.

One day Bellissima was prancing about in front of him. "Sit still," he said, "and you will make a beautiful picture for my collection." But Bellissima would not keep still and the only thing to do was to tie the dog up, at head and tail. The dog barked and jumped up and down, so that the string had to be tightened—and at that moment the Signora came in.

"You unchristian boy! Oh, my poor little dog!" was all she could manage to say, and she pushed the child aside, kicked him and threw him out of the house—he was the most ungrateful, good-for-nothing, the most godless child in the world! Weeping, she kissed the little half-strangled dog.

At that very moment the painter came up the stairs—and this is the turning-point of the story.

In 1834 there was an exhibition in the Academia degli Arti in Florence. Two pictures, hanging side by side, attracted a large number of viewers. The smaller picture showed an attractive small boy sitting sketching. As his model he had a small, close-clipped white poodle, but the dog would not sit still and was therefore tethered with string at both head and tail. There was a liveliness and truth in this picture which appealed to everyone. It was said that the artist was a young Florentine who had been found on the street as a child and brought up by an old glove-maker. He had taught himself to draw. A now famous painter had discovered the boy's talent when the child was being turned out of the house because he had tied up the Signora's darling, the little poodle, in order to use it as a model.

The glove-maker's apprentice had become a great artist, as this picture showed—and this was proved too by the bigger picture beside it. Here there was only one figure, a ragged little boy sleeping in the street on the back of the bronze boar[2] in the Porta Rossa. Everyone knew the place. The child's arm rested on the animal's head: he was sleeping soundly. The lamp under the image of the Virgin Mary on the wall cast a light on the child's pale but lovely face. It was a beautiful picture. It was set in a great gilt frame and at the corner there was a laurel wreath, but between the green leaves was entwined a black ribbon and a long mourning band hung down from it. The young artist had died only a few days before.[3]

---

[2] The bronze boar is a copy. The original is antique and of marble: it stands at the entrance to the gallery in the Palazzo degli Uffizi.

[3] This story was later included in H.C.A.'s Collected Stories. The bronze boar still sits today in the little market at Porta Rossa, and through the grille into the small basin in front of him one throws coins, which are then collected for charity.

My Boots (A TRUE STORY)

December 19, 1840—February 14, 1841, Rome

There is a street in Rome called the Via Purificazione, but one cannot say of it that it is purified! Up and down cabbage-stalks and old potsherds lie strewn all around, smoke oozes out of the tavern door, and every morning the Signora in the house across the way—I have to say it, it is true—this Signora shakes her bedclothes out of the window.

Many foreigners live in this street, but this year fear of the fever and other malignant diseases kept most of them away in Naples and Florence. I was living quite alone in a big house; not even the landlord and his wife slept in at night. It was a large, cold house with a damp little garden in which there was only a row of peas and a half-rotten stock—although in the neighboring gardens, which lay somewhat higher, there were flowering hedges of damask roses and trees thick with yellow lemons. The lemons survived the continuous rain quite well, but the roses looked as if they had been a whole week in the sea.

The evenings were very lonely in the big chilly rooms, the fireplace yawned between the windows, and outside there was rain and rough weather. All the doors were fastened with locks and iron bars, but these were of no avail with the wind whistling sharply through every chink and crevice. Thin sticks blazed up in the fireplace, but they did not send out much warmth. The cold stone floor, the bare walls and the high ceiling seemed to have been intended only for summertime. If for once I wanted to be really comfortable, I had first to put on my wool-lined traveling-boots, then my overcoat, cape and woolly cap—after which I would be quite cozy. To be sure, the side nearest the fire was half-roasted, but in this world one must learn to adapt oneself, and I turned myself around like a sunflower.

The evenings were rather long, but my teeth decided to give a concert on their nerves, and it was remarkable how accomplished their performance was. A solid, plain Danish toothache cannot be compared to an Italian one. The pain played around on all the keys and notes of my teeth, as though a Liszt or Thalberg were sitting at the keyboard. First it rolled in the front, then in the back, like two warlike choirs answering each other, while one of the front teeth sang the *prima donna*'s role, with every painful ornament, trill and high jump. The ensemble was so good and they all performed with such strength that in the end I was no longer human!

The evening performance turned into a night concert and it was during one such, with the windows rattling in the wind and the rain pouring down outside, that I cast a half-sorrowful look at the night lamp. My writing materials stood beside it and I saw, quite clearly, that the pen was dancing over the paper, as if propelled by an unseen hand—but it was not, it was doing it itself. It was taking dictation—but who was dictating? I know it sounds unbelievable, but this is the truth! I declare it and you will believe me—it was my boots, my old Copenhagen boots which, because they were soaked through, had been put on the hearth by the hot embers. If I were racked with pain, they were packed with rain! They were dictating their autobiography, and this I think will throw some light on that Italian winter, *anno* 1840–1841.

The boots said:

"We are two brothers—left foot, right foot. Our first memory is of being well rubbed with wax and then polished and polished. Each of us could see himself mirrored in his brother and his brother was reflected in him. We were one body, like Castor and Pollux or Siamese twins, which fate had decreed should live and die, exist or not exist together, with each other. We were both native-born Copenhageners.

"The shoemaker's boy carried us carefully out into the world, and this aroused sweet but false hopes about our destiny. The man we were brought to at once took us by the ears and pulled until we fitted round his feet and legs—then he went down the stairs and we creaked for

This quiet Roman scene was made in the 1830's; it shows a villa just outside one of the gates of the city. NEW YORK PUBLIC LIBRARY PICTURE COLLECTION.

joy. Although it was raining outside, we went on creaking—but only for that first day.

"Oh dear, what a lot of water there is to go through in this world! We were not born to be waterproof boots and we did not feel happy. No brush could give us back that shine of youth which we had had when the cobbler's lad carried us carefully through the streets. How can we describe our joy when we heard one morning that we were to travel abroad—yes, to Italy, that mild, warm land where we would tread on marble and classical earth, drink in the sun and surely recover our youthful shine.

"We traveled. For much of the journey we slept in a trunk and dreamed about the warm countries. In the towns, however, we took a good look around us—but it was damp and raw, just as in Denmark. Our soles rotted and had to be removed in Munich: we got new ones instead, but they were as well made as if we had been born with them. 'If only we were across the Alps,' we sighed. 'There it is mild and fine.' And we crossed the Alps and it was not mild and fine. It rained and it blew and whenever we trod on marble it was so ice-cold that the stone drew cold sweat out of our soles and we left a wet print where we had trodden!

"It was quite lively in the evenings, when the waiter numbered all the boots and shoes of the hotel guests. We were lined up with all those foreign comrades and they told us all about the places they had come from. There was one pair with beautiful red Moroccan leather uppers and black soles, I think it was in Bologna. They told us about the warm summer in Rome and Naples; they told us about their excursion to Vesuvius, where their feet were burnt through by underground heat. We almost longed to die that same way! If only we were across the Appennines, if only we were in Rome—and then we got there.

"But now we have gone along in rain and mud, one week after another. One has to see everything and there is no end either to sightseeing or to drenching rain. Not one warm ray of sun has refreshed us, only the cold wind has embraced us. Rome! Rome! For the very first time tonight we are drinking in warmth from this blessed fire and we shall drink until we burst! Our soles have gone, we are down on our uppers, and our legs are cracking. But before we die this welcome, happy death, we want this our story to be recorded. We want our remains brought to Berlin to rest by the side of him who had the courage and heart enough to describe *Italien wie es ist*—the truth-loving Nicolai!"

And then the boots collapsed.

It was quite quiet; the lamp went out and I dozed a little. When I woke in the morning I thought it was all a dream, but I looked into the fireplace and the boots were completely shriveled up, they stood like mummies in the cold ashes. I looked at the paper which lay beside the lamp. It was covered with ink blots: the pen had in truth written all over it, but everything had run together because the pen had written the boots' memoirs on wrapping paper.

I wrote down what I could still remember—and you will please note that it was not I who cried WOE! over *la bella Italia*, but my boots.

The gaiety of carnival time in Rome excited Andersen. Here shepherds with bagpipe and horn play country tunes before a religious sanctuary. E.N.I.T.

Carnival in Rome

The last day of Carnival is always the most animated. It ends with the bouquet of the whole festival, the brilliant, beautiful *Moccolo*. This year there was a costumed couple on yard-high stilts; very skillfully they moved between the wagons and the walkers. Here there were two dressed as children, one white, one coal-black, chained to each other and roaring. They were followed by a miller, chained to a chimney-sweep. A man hopped about with lottery tickets, his hat crowned with a balloon. Another came with an organ on a cart, and from each pipe a living cat stuck its head and screeched, for the man had a little string tied round their tails. One wagon was decorated like a throne of flowers and on it sat a minstrel. The harp was anchored, but over it there was a wheel of fortune with a lot of flags. It turned in the wind.

All through the long streets flowers and confetti rained down; mostly flowers, because February this year burgeoned with violets and anemones. I saw Don Miguel—the real Don Miguel himself—wandering in the crowd, in civilian clothes. He got a handful of confetti. Queen Christina of Spain had a seat on a balcony.

Then came the signal for the horse-race—that day one of the spectators was killed by the goaded horses. This happens every year. The body was carried to the side and cheerfulness broke out again. *Moccoli*, *moccoli* re-echoed and at that moment, from all the windows, from every balcony—even from the rooftops—long reeds, sticks and stakes appeared, trimmed with small burning wax papers. The carriage folk who, during the horserace, had to lay by in the side-streets, once again filled the Corso, but the horses, the coachmen's hats, their whips, everything was surrounded by burning wax tapers. Every lady in the carriages carried her light and tried to shield it against the opponent who tried to put it out. Poles with kerchiefs waved in the air. A shouting, a noise of which no one who has not heard it can have any impression, deafens one's ears. *Senza moccolo, senza moccolo.* Small paper balloons with lights inside fluttered down on the crowd: in this incredible street it was as if all the stars of Heaven, not forgetting the Milky Way, were wandering through Il Corso. The air was warmed by the lights, the ears were deafened by the noise. It was the wildest Bacchanal. And then, in a moment, the lights were put out—one saw the last one and then it was dark, it was still. The church bells rang out and the long time of fasting began.

The next morning one well-packed carriage after another drove away with the foreigners—away from Rome, now deathly quiet, where all the galleries are closed, all the pictures on the altars covered with black sheets. And we are on our way to Naples.

Departure From Italy

March 15, 1841

My trunk and overnight bag, packed full and locked, stood in the middle of my room, and the porter was on his way up the stairs to take the things down. I was leaving Naples, leaving Italy—and I was glad. How people change! When I left this country last time I was very sad and depressed, although then my journey was home to the North and now I was on my way to Greece and the Orient.

I hope I shall be forgiven if, for a few moments, I think about myself—but only for so long as it takes the porter to carry my luggage down the stairs.

I have earlier given descriptions of Italy that almost, I think, breathe the sunlight and beauty of this country. Now, on the other hand, many of my pictures have dark shadows—but this is how I have seen Italy this time. The scent of novelty had gone! The winter was unusually hard and I was personally sick, both spiritually and physically. Here in Naples, a few days ago, fever was burning in my blood. Perhaps I was near to death—I think that death looked in at the door, but it was not yet time, and he went away and the Goddess of Health stood there in his place. Outside, spring came just as suddenly, the snow round the hills melted and the sea lay smooth and blue. A new journey, a new life perhaps was beginning.

March 17–18, 1841, Malta

A hopeful crowd of Moors flocked around us at the landing-stage, all offering their services as guide. We chose one to take us as far as the Hotel de' Mediterraneo. He was clad in rags, but he wore them as proudly as a prince his purple—two black eyes flashed in his brown face.

A drawbridge leads to the gate of Valletta, and inside the gate begins a street of fruit shops. Fruit of every kind that is found in the South meets the eye, a sight so rich and varied as one never sees in the North. There was a movement and a throng of people here like that in Toledo Street in Naples—Maltese women all in black and with veils held so tightly around their heads that one could see only their eyes and nose, English soldiers in their red uniforms, ragged good-for-nothings and braided sailors, all busily on the move. Handsome carriages with two wheels and only one horse trotted past, a Moorish groom running by the side.

Soon we were in broader streets: All the houses looked palatial—notable features were the green-painted, wooden balcony bay windows, with which they were decorated. All the main streets were airy and broad, some macadamized, some paved with lava. But everything was very clean, one might almost say festive.

The hotel into which we went was as comfortable and handsome as if it had been brought here from Queen Victoria's royal capital. I was sitting with a French newspaper in my hands when I heard a noise outside. My Russian traveling companion had offered our Moor only a few pence for his walk with us and the fellow would not accept so little. I saw how much the sum was and thought too that it should be increased. The Russian said no and opened the door, the Moor laid the money on the step, put his foot on it and with a look that would have made an impression on any stage, expressed his Pride and Anger. I wanted to give him more money, but the Russian placed himself between us, gave the waiters a nod, and they pushed the malcontent outside. And that, for them, was the end of the story.

Immediately afterwards I went into the street where I expected to find the Moor, and there indeed he stood, surrounded by a crowd of ragged fellows. The money which the waiter had put outside the door still lay there in the same place. I proffered about three times as much as he had been offered, giving him to understand that it came from me. His eyes rolled in his head, he pointed again at the miserable coins the other had offered him, pointed to his rags, held my arm back away from him—he would accept Nothing. He shook his fist at the house and stalked off, proud as an injured aristocrat. I was depressed by this first incident in Malta.

Towards evening we went on board our ship again. The scene over the water and the life there was a play I shall never forget. As the sun sank, cannon salutes sounded and all the flags on our ship came down. It was only a few minutes and then night lay over us, without twilight, but night as it comes in the South, clear and transparent with twinkling stars, stars that say, "We are suns, can you doubt it?"

The traffic faded and was lost in the city. A faint sound of music wafted over to us, but soon got louder, in strong tones from the two warships which lay nearest to us. "God save the Queen" was played and sung as I have never heard it before, but the surroundings played their part too. And now there was the sound of dance music—there was a ball on one of the ships. The stars themselves seemed to dance, mirrored in the water. The boats rocked gently, and it was late before I could tear myself away from this sight.

Early the next morning I was woken by the sound of cleaning-up after the coal had been taken on board. When I came up, the deck shone in all its freshness and we were getting ready to sail. All around us there were shouts and cries, the floating shops with their merchants ringed us about, naked boys begged, passengers were coming on board. Our Persian passenger sat on a sack of coal near to the funnel. A Bedouin swathed in his white burnoose and with pistols and knives in his belt lay with his back to him; a couple of Maltese women in their black veils had grouped themselves near to the engines; Greeks in colored dress and with the red fez on their heads were leaning against the gunwale. By the gangplank two sailors stood guard, with iron-bound halberds. Packages, crates and chests were piled up. The mate's whistle sounded, steam puffed out of the funnel and around the ship's wheel. There was a sound of cannon-fire, flags waved and smoothly we glided out, away from the quay, out to the open Mediterranean which lay as blue and still as a velvet cloth stretched out over the earth. The sea seemed to be only a blue veil, a starless heaven beneath us, stretching out in the transparent air as far as the eye could see, far, far beyond anything I have seen before. There seemed to be no horizon—sea and sky were fused into one, with a clarity and into an infinity that cannot be described and could not be comprehended other than in the depths of one's own thoughts and imagination.

Part Two

GREECE

A Couple of Days in the Mediterranean

March 18, 1841, from Malta to Syra, Greece

The open sea was dead calm; there was no movement at all to be felt in the ship—one could wander up or down, as though on dry land. Only by looking at the wake could one see the ship's progress, ever farther and farther away from the yellow cliffs of Malta.

We had taken on board seven young Spanish monks who knew little Italian, were all missionaries and were now on their way to India. The youngest of them was very handsome, pale and melancholy; he told me that his parents were still alive and that he had not seen his mother since he was sixteen. She was very dear to him—"and now I shall not see her until we meet in heaven," he sighed. It was with a heavy and bleeding heart that he was leaving Europe, but he recognized that he must; he was called upon to do so, since he was in God's service. He and the other six brothers all belonged to the Teresian Order.

For most of the people on board I was the one who appeared to have come from the farthest away—I came from the North. "From Denmark!" repeated a cleric from Rome, who was going to Jerusalem. "Denmark! So you are American?"

I explained that Denmark was a long way from America, but he shook his head like the lady in *The Danes in Paris* and said, like her, "Not all that far, not all that far!"

We had on board a Papal Nuncio who was going to Lebanon; he was the only one of the Italians who knew a little about Denmark: He knew there was someone called Thorvaldsen and that there had been a man called Tycho Brahe.[1] I have since noted that Tycho Brahe

---

[1] Tycho Brahe (1546–1601) was a Danish astronomer, who established his famous observatory of Uraniborg on the island of Hveen in 1576, but was forced into exile in 1597 after losing royal protection. His astronomical observations included precise notation of planetary and stellar positions.

is the Dane by whom Denmark is the most known; Tycho is our most famous countryman—and we exiled him! Denmark is a great mother, but she is sometimes not a good mother to her best children.

Towards midday we could still see Malta; of Sicily on the other hand we could see only snow-capped Etna, but it was vast and clear, shining like a white pyramid of sun-lit marble. There was no swell in the sea; it was as if we were gliding through the air. An enormous dolphin, bigger than any horse, rolled itself a couple of times up near to the ship, the sun shining on its wet, glistening back. Tunes from *The White Lady*[2] floated up to us from the piano down in the salon and the cheerful sailors hung in the rigging and sang "Quel plaisir d'être matelot!"

The captain's pipe shrilled, the crew did their maneuvers. The dinner-bell rang. As we were drinking our coffee the sun sank, vast and red and the sea glowed like fire. . . .

At nine o'clock I was already in my bunk and went straight to sleep while the ship pursued its unaltered speed and course ahead. When early in the morning I went up on deck again, it was being cleaned. All hands were at work and soon the deck was shining, white and clean, so that it was a pleasure to see. Up where the anchors and ropes lay, the crew were doing their laundry and this was a remarkable sight. They took particular care of their trousers—they spread them out on the deck, threw seawater over them and then brushed or rather scrubbed them, just as they were, with an ordinary broom which was rather the worse for wear and among the spines of which they had stuck a piece of soap.

Two sturdy sailor boys, quite small but lively as squirrels and full of tricks, were killing hens and before each killing they made a humorous speech to the bird—the speech always ended with a "Voila!" and the knife went to the throat.

Astern the sailors were having their breakfast; each had a ration of wine, onions and bread. They were all very cheerful—they had their leading humorist and one who was the butt for their humor.

---

[2] *The White Lady—La Dame Blanche* by F. A. Boieldieu (1775–1834), a successful light opera with libretto by Scribe, based on Sir Walter Scott's *The Monastery* and *Guy Mannering*.

The Persian in the green caftan and white "shawled" turban, sat always alone and played with his earrings or his saber; no one spoke to him and he spoke to no one but now and again a smile played around his lips as though happy memories were going through his mind, or perhaps he was thinking of his homecoming, of the many things he had to tell from land and sea. As I went by him he suddenly gripped my arm, said something in Persian which I did not understand, but he laughed, nodded and pointed to the side of the deck. My friendly morning greeting he repaid by drawing my attention to a little incident that was happening on our flight over the sea. A tiny bird had wearily lighted on the rigging and now glided down on deck. It was so exhausted that it could no longer flutter its wings. There were quickly a lot of spectators and I was very angry with the cleric from Rome, when he immediately wanted it cooked—he was sure it would taste very good.

"Our little pilgrim shall not be eaten," I said; one of the lieutenants took it into his care, put it onto the canvas that was spread like a tent over the first class, gave it a saucer of water and some breadcrumbs. The bird was our guest for the whole of that day and indeed night too and only the next day did it fly from the ship—chirrupping in its flight as though it would say thank you for its good treatment.

It was a great event for us all; but soon afterwards each of us returned to his own occupation—one to the piano, another to his book, some played cards, others walked up and down. The Bedouin sat on the sacks of coal, silent as a ghost; his eyes flashed in his brown face under the white burnoose, his bare dark-brown legs stretched out in front of him. The Persian played with his great saber, stroked his pistols or twisted the silver rings in his dark brown ears. The Captain copied from my album a picture by *Marstrand*.[3] *Only a Fiddler* now lives in the Captain's cabin and every year the Fiddler sails between Marseilles and Constantinople on the proud ship *Leonidas*. As for me, I read German with one of the French officers; he translated Schiller's *The*

---

[3] Wilhelm Marstrand (1810–1873) was a Danish painter who was in Munich in 1840 and then was a member of the Danish colony in Rome. He was later a professor at the Danish Academy. *Only a Fiddler* was the title of a successful novel (1837) by Andersen.

Division of the World. The time passed most enjoyably; at the dinner table there was good humor and merriment.

We could still see Mount Etna to the northwest, otherwise there was only the endless sea. But at dinner time, I saw in the northeast a white patch which could not be a ship—it was too broad for that, but it was perhaps a cloud. I thought it might be the coast of Greece and asked the Captain about it. He shook his head and said that only the next day should we be able to see Greece, which right enough lay over where I thought I could already see land. Neither he nor any of the other passengers saw anything.

After dinner, shortly before sunset, I looked in the same direction as before; it shone out just as clearly as Etna! No—it could not be a cloud, it had not changed its form, and was still there in the same place as three hours earlier.

The Captain took his telescope and shouted "Land!"

Yes—it was the coast of Greece; it was a mountain top at Navarino; snow-topped it glistened in the clear air. It was I who first of all of them had discovered Greece!

"Never have I heard before," said the Captain, "that anyone with the naked eye, at one and the same time has been able to see from the Mediterranean both Etna and the Greek coast. It is amazing!"

When I told this story later in Athens, a scholar said that recently in a review of an English work he had read of this same curious feature, but the critic had expressed serious doubts about it. But it is a fact and I have seen it myself. Snow on Mount Etna and snow on Greek mountains in the clear sunlight at that point makes it possible to see the land both to the east and west.

The next morning I was up before dawn; it was the 20th of March. Blood-red, as I have never before seen it and wonderfully oval in shape, the sun rose, daylight spread over the dead calm sea and before us to the right lay, clear and distinct, but still a long way away, the coast of the Morea. It was the ancient Lacedaemon that we could see. A steep wall of rock went straight down, vertically into the sea and inland there rose up the snow-covered, picturesque hills! How my heart rejoiced!

A Panorama of South Morea and the Cyclades

March 21–22, 1841

We were approaching the Morea—the name means Mulberryland and it is so called after its appearance, which is like a mulberry leaf. Across it the river Eurotas runs and there lay ancient Sparta, where the grave of Agamemnon is to be found. These same mountain shapes—with the same sunlight and shadows as we now see them—were seen by the Phoenicians and Pelasgians,[1] the waves broke then as they do now for us. The whole scene is unchanged. We sailed close in under the rock face of Cape Matapan—the entire coast seemed to be bare and without vegetation. The waves broke high against the cliffs, where no mountain goats climbed, where there was no sight of a shepherd or huntsman. But in this very bare wilderness each plot and patch has a value, an interest far greater than we sometimes feel for the richest landscape—because this was Greece!

We passed the outer point of the land of the *Maniots*,[2] that Spartan race who were never conquered, a folk brave and bold, coarse and wild, but hospitable as in the days of Lycurgus.

The sea was now running high—there was a wind off the mountains; the Morea stretched its bare Cape Malea out into the foaming surf. How wild and deserted, how solitary it looked. And here there was a human dwelling, a hermit's cell, quite cut off from the world, surrounded by screaming seabirds, close by the sea. It was impossible, even with a telescope, to discover a cliff path by which people could make their way down to the hermit.

The hut was low and small, it had a hole for the door and window. Close by a human being was moving about; it was the hermit of Cape

---

[1] Pelasgians were an ancient people of the Aegean who were referred to in both *The Iliad* and *The Odyssey* of Homer.

[2] The name "Maniot" comes from the Greek word *mania* (madness/anger) and indicates the wildness with which they attack their enemies. HCA.

41

Malea—the first human being we saw on the coast of Greece! Who was he? What had driven him out into this wild solitude? No one answered our question. He and his hut have been seen here for many years. Ships, each with its little enclosed world, glide by; he looks at them as at pictures in a dream, he looks at them as he looks at the white gulls; he recites his morning and evening prayers when the sea is calm and when, in a storm, it sings its mighty chorale.

We drew farther and farther away. Towards the northwest a rock shaped like a gigantic helmet rose up out of the sea, tinged by the red rays of the evening sun. I took it for an outpost of the Cyclades, but we were to reach these only during the night.

At early dawn I was on deck again; a couple of sailing boats cruised by, close up to us, like enormous seabirds that would strike our rigging with their white wings.

High up to the heavens bare rock masses towered from the water—this was the island of Melos, which is hollowed out by fire and water, with Siphanto, Seriphos and Thera. We sailed as in a canal between the last two. Magnetic mines lie under the stone-crust, sweet scented roses grow on top, but the passing traveler sees nothing of this; the coast shows itself bare and wild.

The sun rose behind the mountains of the island of Mykonos; it lit up Paros and Anti-Paros, but no slopes of marble shone here. The gray rocks lay dead and heavy in the water. There was nothing to give us any impression at all of the mighty stalactite grotto with its wonders. We saw the cliffs of Naxos where Ariadne had wept, where the Maenads, with their hair flowing over their lovely shoulders, danced in the star-clear nights and sang their hymns to Bacchus; but the high mountains hid from us the fertile, wine growing valleys. Ida, the holy mountain of Zeus, pointed solemnly towards that heaven from which mortals have banished the old gods.

The ship steered its course towards a small island on which there stood a slender white lighthouse, and as soon as we had passed this the harbor of Syra opened before us. Curved like a horseshoe around the bay lay the town, with shining white houses, rather like a camp of tents on the gray hillside. It was exactly like a miniature Naples;

the Bishop's palace here high on the mountain reminded one of St. Elmo. I had imagined all Greek towns as only ruins and clay huts, but the town on Syra looked both picturesque and inviting.

A whole fleet of Greek boats were rowed out to us and lay to leeward by the side of our ship, but all the same they were continually rolling together because the sea was running high. I let my baggage slide down into one of the nearest boats and then jumped after it; from the steamer a "farewell" came to me from the friends I had so quickly made on board and whom I should now probably never see again in this world—a thought that made me sad.

The sailors started rowing towards land, but we were a long way out. The waves rocked our boat as if it were an orange skin; it was in danger of overturning in the heavy swell and we were sprayed with foam. But finally we came into the harbor where ship lay by ship, one close by the next.

The whole quay was thronged with Greeks, with tight jackets, white *fustanella*[3] and red caps on their heads. There was much shouting and screaming. An old man stretched out his hand to me with welcome, and I stood on Greek soil. Gratitude to God, joy at being here and yet a certain feeling of being alone and desolate filled me at that moment.

At the office of the French Steamship Company I learned that the Austrian steamer would arrive only in seven days' time; the Greek ship had broken down and was out of action. But there was an opportunity for me to leave the same day, if I were prepared to begin my arrival in Piraeus with a few days' quarantine. The French warship *Lycurgus*, which had come from Alexandria—where at that moment the plague was raging—had been lying for some weeks under the quarantine flag by Syra and would sail that very evening to Piraeus and there end its quarantine in three days' time. I immediately took a boat and was once again out on the unquiet sea, being rowed out to the *Lycurgus* where the green flag was flying. My luggage was flung into an empty boat which was hanging on a rope by the ship's ladder—

---

[3] Fustanella is the name for the pleated skirt worn by men in the Greek national dress.

the sailors hauled it up and my belongings were on board. And now at last I could return to explore the town.

Close by the quay there was an open wooden shop with a clay floor and crude beams supporting a ceiling which covered half the room; the other half had only the roof as cover. It was a café. All around at small wooden tables sat Greeks and foreigners. Over a brazier stood the coffee pot; a handsome Greek boy stirred it with a stick that he twisted with both hands so that the coffee was uniformly thick and then he poured it, boiling hot, into the cup.[4] Two Russian sailors were dancing to a dreadful violin played by an old Greek.

I went farther into the town; the streets were very narrow and in the main one, which wound around the bay, there was shop after shop, each like an upturned box—here were sold articles of clothing, the fez, Moroccan leather shoes, fruit and food. In front of the *Hotel della Grece*, on a wooden balcony painted in motley colors, sat Greeks and oriental-clad people, all with long pipes. I met only one foreigner. He was a Russian who straightway asked me what I was doing in this confounded country, among these people. "All of them are scoundrels," he said, "accursed be all those writers, those Lamartines[5] who describe these places so that one wants to visit them! Would I had one of those gentlemen here—I'd break every bone in his body! I've just come from Constantinople traveling along the coast and was robbed by the Albanians. Every stitch of clothing have they taken from me and they killed my servant. I sit here and wait for money and letters of credit. It is an infamous country and bad people. What do *you* want in the Orient!" It was a very pleasant reception!

However, I went over to a barber nearby and sat myself down on a wooden bench by the wall among the others—Greeks. A leather strap that hung fast to the wall was put around my neck and the sharp blade flew light as a feather over my face, which was then sprinkled

---

[4] Coffee in Greece and the Orient is quite excellent—indeed so good that the traveler who comes from these countries can at first find no taste in coffee made in the ordinary European way. One drinks it "thick"—the coffee is quite smooth, but it is not ground, it is pounded to a powder, just like chocolate. HCA.

[5] A reference to Alphonse de Lamartine's *Souvenirs d'un Voyage en Orient 1835*. HCA read this in Danish before setting out on this journey. He met Lamartine in Paris in 1843.

with eau de cologne. The barber asked if I were an Englishman and when I said I was Danish he clasped me to his bosom and said, "Bravo Americano!" Once again I protested that I was not American but Danish—but he nodded happily, laid his hand on his heart and explained, as I understood him, how dear to all Greeks the Americans were from the time of the War of Liberation, when the American ships brought them supplies.

I wandered through the streets which were thronged with people, but I saw not one Greek woman. The windows in all the houses were covered from the inside with blinds or long curtains. Soon I found myself in less crowded streets, which lay higher up on the side of the mountains. In front of most of the houses here there was a kind of forecourt, with an arbor made of a single vine. Flower-pots stood by the walls and on the flat roofs of the houses. The road before individual houses was paved in mosaic, the stones forming stars and scrolls.

I went into the main church which, compared with the Italian ones I had seen in Malta, was small and insignificant; but on the other hand, as compared with churches in Greece generally it could be regarded as considerable. The altar panels gleamed with gilding and icons; great silver lamps hung in rows the length and breadth of the church. A couple of small boys were playing inside. My thoughts were turned to prayer. . . .

The highest part of the town was still under construction; the road was like a path through a stone quarry—fragments and lumps of mountain rock lay all about where the houses were being built. But the view was beautiful over the town and harbor, towards the little island with its slender white lighthouse. On the opposite side of the bay was the quarantine station. I saw the islands of Tenos, Delos and Naxos and the top of Andros. As I looked out towards these islands a steamer went by—I recognized the flag; it was the *Leonidas*. It disappeared round the coast of Delos. "Farewell, farewell!" I shouted, but no one heard me; the ship was gone. I saw only the smoke, which was lying like a cloud between the islands.

Towards evening I went out to the *Lycurgus*. The sea ran high; two cheerful Greeks rowed, shouting with glee every time the sea lifted up the boat so that we were very nearly thrown overboard. Strange faces welcomed me on board. At sundown we weighed anchor and the ship steamed northeast around Syra, where we found smooth waters. It was a lovely star-clear evening. I had not yet met anyone; I sat on the plinth of a cannon and looked at the beautiful sky. A foreign, eastern-clad man was standing with his back to me. He turned, I looked at him, he looked at me, nodded in a friendly way and touched his turban. It was the Persian with whom I had sailed from Naples. We two were the only old comrades from the *Leonidas*—he seemed to be glad to see me, just as I was to see him. He too was going to Athens and from there home. He offered me fruit; I offered him some in return, but neither of us could make ourselves understood in words. I pointed towards the lovely starry sky; he touched his turban. I thought that I must say something, if only a flow of words of a language that was related to his. What else did I know other than the first line of Genesis in Hebrew; one does what one can to help! I pointed to the stars and said: *"Bereschit Barah Elohim Et Haschamaim Veet Haaretz!"*[6] And he smiled, nodded and also wanted to say all that he knew of a tongue that he thought was mine: "Yes Sir, verily, verily!"

That was the sum total of our conversation. Neither of us knew any more—but what good friends we were!

---

[6] "In the beginning God created the Heaven and the Earth." In Andersen's day some elementary Hebrew was part of the Latin (Grammar) School curriculum in Denmark.

The Bay of Piraeus and Arrival in Athens

Early next morning I heard the anchor drop; I went up on deck. We lay in the bay of Piraeus, which looked like a small inlet. Behind the mountains of the island of Aegina there rose the still higher mountains of Morea, each one bolder than the other. Two floating barrels served as buoys in the rather narrow entrance to the inlet, and at night each carried a light like a beacon. I counted about 130 houses in Piraeus; behind them and behind stony, yellow earth and gray-green olive trees Lykabettos rose up and the lower-lying Acropolis. The mountains Hymettos and Pentelikon completed the panorama, which has a stony, hard appearance, "stony Attica" as the ancients used to say. To the left lay a small peninsula with a few bushes, a high-lying windmill and the new quarantine building; to the right a bare stony plain stretched out towards the mountains of Parnes.

In this bay, where Themistocles launched sixty galleys every year, there now lay only a couple of small Greek ships and one boat but, on the other hand, a number of large English, French and Austrian vessels, as well as two steamships in addition to ours. Some smartly dressed Greeks rowed past us and later in the morning there came a boat with Danes on board, who bade me welcome. There was much to hear, many questions to answer. Danish tongues spoke of their love for Denmark, their enthusiasm for Greece—but we could speak only at a distance, for our ship was in quarantine. . . . . .

March 24–April 20, 1841, Athens

On the third morning in Piraeus the hour of our freedom struck. I think there lay a dozen Greek boats around our ship. I sprang into the first and best and with strong strokes of the oars our sailors made for land, we found waiting a great many four-wheelers, old coaches and open wagons, all of which seemed to have served their time,

47

perhaps in Italy and now, in their old age, to have emigrated to Greece in order to work again. It was only a couple of years ago that between Piraeus and Athens there stretched a swamp around which went camels loaded with goods, but now there is an excellent highway and a *khan*[1] where one can get refreshments. For a mere bagatelle one drives along this road, which is about one Danish mile. All our luggage was loaded into an old coach, which was almost completely filled up; trunks and traveling bags peered out of both windows. The company itself was in three large wagons—at the back of the one in which I sat we had a gaily dressed Greek, the porter from the *Hotel du Munich* in Athens. He was so well and richly dressed that, at a masquerade in the North, he could well have passed for an Hellenic prince.

We rolled joyfully out of Piraeus. Sailors with shiny hats were sitting outside cafés, which really looked to me like large rooms made of planks; a "hurrah" was given for us as the wineglasses were emptied. The road went over the remains of the ancient walls, which had been built from a kind of yellow stone, still found at the bottom of the cliffs here. We went at a gallop which raised a fearful dust—but anyway it was classical dust!

Soon we reached the olive grove, the sacred grove of Minerva. There was a wooden stall on each side of the road; lemons and oranges were on display, garnished with a row of bottles of wine and liqueurs. While our horses were given fresh water here, beggars came up with their tin bowls and we gave them all something—they were after all Greeks.

As in the great days of Athens, one now hurries from Piraeus through the great olive wood. Before us lay the Acropolis, which I had so often seen in pictures, but now it was there in reality! Steep Lykabettos with its shining white hermitage stood out very distinctly—I could see Athens! A few steps from the city, close by the road on the right, stands the Temple of Theseus, so unspoiled and grand with its beautiful marble columns which have become golden brown with age. I actually saw it!

---

[1] A *khan* is a caravansary or rest house in the Middle East.

I could not really believe that I was here in Greece, that I was really rolling into Minerva's city. Hermes Road is the biggest in Athens and is also the first for the traveler coming in from Piraeus; but it begins with a row of houses which, by European standards, look very wretched and poor. Little by little one saw there were better and bigger houses of two stories as in the town on Syra; all the same, to me at least, there was something here that said, "Here is the capital of Greece." The Acropolis stood like a gigantic throne high over all the small houses and in the middle of the street where we drove there was a palm tree—taller than I have ever seen before. A little barrier of crude planks surrounded the trunk, otherwise it would have been wrecked by the Greeks driving by, who stood up in their ancient carriages and chased by as if in a horse race. Of everything around us, this palm tree attracted the most attention; later I learned that when the road was made the tree ought to have been cut down because it stood just where people would drive, but our fellow-countryman, Professor Ross from Holstein, pleaded for the palm and it was allowed to remain there. I therefore called it "Ross's Palm" and all travelers and travel-writers have since called it the same.[2]

We urge the Greeks to remember that their country forms the bridge between Europe and the Orient. They should preserve the oriental decorations and things that exemplify this—and an outstanding example is this palm tree. Most of the others in Athens have been destroyed; there are only two or three left.

We stopped at the *Hotel du Munich*; the host was Greek, his wife German; she was called "Die Schöne Wienerinn." They gave me the best room and it was just like one finds in every little German town in a third class hostelry. But anyway, I now had a home, a home in Athens.

---

[2] Ludwig Ross (1806–1859) was an archeologist, born in Holstein. He was in Greek service from 1832 to 1843 and was a professor in Athens. Andersen saw much of him during his visit to Greece.

March 24–April 20, 1841, Athens

I shall try to give my first impressions of the city itself and to recount how I spent the first day. The dreadful picture that I had been given in Naples of Greece and particularly of Athens I found to be exaggerated to the point of laughter, but I would be prepared to believe that six or seven years ago everything here was in a very wretched state. But one must remember what just one year alone can mean to a country such as Greece, which is in a period of change and development like no other in Europe. It is as if one would compare this remarkable progress in the intellectual sense in a child, with the less striking progress in the grown man. Seven months for the one are the equivalent of about seven years in the other. Athens struck me as being about the same size as a Danish provincial town, for example Helsingør, and it looked like a place that had been hurriedly put up for a fair that was now in full swing. What here are called bazaars are crooked, ordinary streets with wooden houses on both sides, wooden booths as in a Danish market that are decorated with scarves, colored stockings, clothes and leather slippers, all a bit muddled up together, but colorful to look at. Here there was meat, and there fruit, brightly colored fezzes and old and new books. Even the coach-driver bought one—and what a book it was! A copy of Homer's *Iliad*, it was printed in Athens in 1839—I read the title myself.

Athens has a few Greek, or rather Turkish, cafés, as well as a new Italian one, so large and ornate that it would in no way be out of place in Hamburg or Berlin. Compared with this, the much frequented Café Greco in Rome is only a sandpit under the stairs! Young Greeks, all in national costume—but so tightly laced that they must have been black and blue around their ribs—with eye-glasses and patent leather gloves, were smoking cigars here and playing billiards. They were real Greek dandies—they only needed to change their costumes to be loungers idling away in any other European capital. Outside on the street corner stood Maltese porters, a whole row of them, standing in the sun like out-of-works on a street corner in Copenhagen.

The most populated area of Athens is that part stretching up to the

Acropolis, but all around a lot of building is going on. Athens is a city that seems to grow even in the few days that a stranger is here. The King's new palace is between the city and Hymettus; it is a marble building for which every stone has been quarried from nearby Pentelikon. The entrance hall is much decorated and hung with portraits of the Greek heroes of the War of Liberation.[3] The University is in the process of construction and it is a Dane (Christian Hausen) who is responsible for the building. A few churches and many private houses for Ministers and merchants grow hour by hour. But who are all the artisans? They are nearly all Greeks, I was told; they are farmers, soldiers, brigands, who have grabbed the trowel, the hammer and the saw—they have seen the foreign workmen and have immediately become builders, smiths and carpenters. The Greeks are an intelligent people.

All in all my first impression of Athens was better than I had been led to expect—from what I had heard in Naples. I said this to Ross and he told me about a Greek from Chios—the island where Homer was born—who is now here in Athens. He was a man who, from his occupation and surroundings, could be called very cultured, but he had never before seen a big city and he was therefore quite amazed by the size and all the luxury he found in the capital of Greece. He constantly expressed his wonder at what he saw, and when someone suggested that, presumably, he now knew Athens by heart, he burst out "By heart? One is never finished with such a place. There is always something new to see and hear! So many amusements, so many comforts! There are carriages to drive in and every day lovely music in front of the King's palace—here there are cafés with newspapers, theaters where they sing and speak—it is a wonderful town!"

The modern size and luxury of Athens overwhelmed him; I found it fairly good, as compared with what I had heard about it; thus one judges from different standards, depending on habit and viewpoint.

---

[3] The War of Liberation was to free Greece from the rule of the Ottoman Empire which had ruled Greece since the 15th century. The decisive battle was fought at Navarino in 1827; the combined forces of British, French and Russians destroyed the Turkish and Egyptian fleets. The Treaty of Adrianople in 1830 established Greek independence. After their first president, Capodistrias, was assassinated, King Otto, a Bavarian, was placed on the throne.

I had expected that I should feel very much a stranger and foreigner in Greece, so far away from home, but in fact I felt very much at home. My fellow countrymen and the Germans were very kind to me. Already, on the first day, I was met and taken to a completely Danish house, by the Queen's chaplain, Lüth from Holstein, who is married to a girl from Fredensborg; her younger sister was staying with them. The house was a center for our compatriots and I met there our Danish Consul, a Dutchman called Travers, who spoke very good Danish. The champagne corks popped.

I was to finish my first day in Athens with a visit to the theater. The theater lies a little outside the town; it has four stories and is beautifully decorated—although the most decorative sights were the Greek-clad spectators in the boxes and the stalls. There were many beautiful Greek women, but I was told that they were all from the islands; not many beauties were to be found in Athens. An Italian company was performing here; the leading singer had recently been hissed off the stage by a cabal and I heard the understudy, who was quite unremarkable. The performance itself was a mish-mash: we had the overtures from *Norma* and *The Bronze Horse*, one act of the *Barber of Seville* and one act of *The Magpie*, as well as a ballet.

From the pit we went into a kind of foyer where one could get refreshments, but out here there were no decorations—everywhere there were only raw beams, wooden planks fixed together; the long counter was also of unplaned boards, where some Greeks were serving punch, almond-milk and coffee.

As I said, the theater lies some way out of town and it therefore gave one a wonderful feeling to come out of this building in the middle of the night from performances of *The Barber* and *The Magpie* and to find oneself under an oriental heaven. The stars were so bright that one could see the wide stretch of desert plain, bounded by high mountains; it was still and solitary here; one could believe that one was in a folk theater in Vienna, bewitched and carried to a desert place by a "powerful spirit." The magnificent natural decoration made the painted scenery seem ridiculous; solitude proclaimed a drama that showed how petty everything was in the place we had just come from.

It was just in the poverty, the wretchedness of this contrast that I felt the whole classical greatness of Greece.

A single marble column stood by our path in rubble and weeds; no one knew which temple it had adorned. Tradition says that it was this column to which Christ was bound when He was flogged; the peasants believe that the Turks cast it into the sea, but that every night it comes back to this place. Solitary this white column stood in the star-clear night pointing up toward God's heaven.

The Acropolis

This isolated, detached rock with its marble ruins is the heart of ancient Athens; its memories stretch back into the age of mythology.[1]

Every path here is historic; every step one treads *is* on ground sacred with memories. The mighty rock to the left, which seems to have been broken loose from the Acropolis by some great natural forces, is the place where the Apostle Paul spoke to the Athenians; now a solitary shepherd sat there with his two dogs and looked over the broad plain where the olives grow. But I gave this picture only a fleeting glance, my eyes moving quickly over the cliff face with the quarried steps to the place where Solon and Plato had spoken—the Acropolis was the goal for my walk, the Acropolis occupied all my thoughts; the wide sea and the picturesque mountains of Morea took my attention only for a moment.

Through an open gateway, with the old iron-barred door hanging on one hinge, I entered the fortress wall which dates from the Turkish era. A couple of inscribed marble grave-stones served as cornices for the entrance. Immediately below, with high arches of enormous free-stones forming a semi-circle, lies the so-called Theater of Herodes.

I had still to go through a little forecourt made up of the ruins of the defense works. A twist of rope hung on the wretched gate, the wooden latch sprang up and I stood in a somewhat larger courtyard where a small guard-house had been built of pieces of broken marble columns, mutilated bas-reliefs and bricks. Half-dressed Greek soldiers, some with rough military coats thrown loosely over their shoulders, lay about in different groups, smoking cigarettes. One was playing a mandolin and singing a Greek song. A few steps more and the path

---

[1] 1400 years before the birth of Christ, Cecrops took a colony from Sais to Greece and on the mountain rock here raised the citadel, Cecropia. The graves of Cecrops and Erechtheus are found here. In the time of Pericles the present Parthenon was built by Phidias and the master builders Ictinus and Callicrates. When Aaron's rod bloomed into flower, Athena's laurel tree put forth young shoots and Neptune's salt spring gushed forth from the rock. HCA.

went on between piled up blocks of marble and overthrown columns. The Temple of the Wingless Goddess of Victory, the mighty Propylaea and a decaying Gothic tower from the Middle Ages lay before us.

This ascent is, and always has been, the only way up to the Acropolis; on all sides the rocks rise steeply and strong walls at the top made it the more inaccessible.

I walked through the colonnade and was now standing in a square that was disordered, wretched to a degree I have never before seen. It was as if an earthquake had shaken the gigantic columns and cornices, one against the other. There was really no longer any way or path here. I walked over blocks of ruined mud huts from the time of the Turks, with grass and acanthus growing between; here and there were the remains of cisterns, here and there wooden sheds in which human bones had been thrown and where vases, basreliefs and plaster casts were stored. Here lay rusty, exploded bombs from the Venetian time.[2] A few horses were grazing up here; and to the left, as in a pit of rubbish, there was the Temple of Erechtheus with its caryatids. A tumble-down brick column filled the place of one caryatid which Elgin had stolen for the British Museum.[3] The skeleton of a donkey was lying in front of the excavated marble steps. A little to the right was the Parthenon, the most glorious ruin on the Acropolis which with its grandeur, its architecture and its reliefs still amazes! It is the temple of all temples: every column has been barbarically broken, every basrelief at the front and on the frieze has been mutilated, and yet it is incredible how much still remains. During the siege by the Venetians part of it exploded with the powder magazine and in the War of Liberation the Parthenon was the target for cannon balls and bombs. And yet these remains still have a grandeur that can only be com-

---

[2] The Venetians invaded the Peloponese in 1687. They destroyed the Parthenon at Athens with gunfire, but did not succeed in taking Greece from the Ottoman Empire.
[3] Lord Elgin: Thomas Bruce, the 7th Earl of Elgin was British Ambassador to Turkey from 1798 to 1803. He is remembered for having acquired a collection of Greek antiquities (with agreement from Constantinople) that became known as the "Elgin Marbles." The collection was derived chiefly from the Parthenon of Athens. Upon his return to England he became the subject of great controversy, some claiming he had saved the ancient art from destruction, and others saying that he had plundered Greece. Eventually the collection was purchased by England for £ 35,000. They now may be viewed in the British Museum.

Greeks Working in the Ruins of the Acropolis, by Martinus Rør-
bye. When Andersen saw the Acropolis several years after this
painting was made, he described it as "disordered and wretched
. . . as if an earthquake had shaken the gigantic columns and
cornices, one against the other." STATENS MUSEUM FOR KUNST,
COPENHAGEN

prehended if one stands here between these magnificent columns,
which bear enormous blocks of marble as though they were only
lightweight rafters. A tumble-down mosque lies across the temple and
now serves as a shed for the marble busts of gods and emperors. On
the side which faces the sea, time has given the columns a red-gold
tinge, but most of them stand just as white as if they had been carved
this year out of Paros's marble quarries.

A few steps away from me, among the broken marble blocks between
which wild thistles had sprung, lay human bones; someone had thrown
down a skull on a white block of marble. . . .

The wind whistled through the colonnades; black birds of prey flew
over the valley towards Hymettos. Just below the rock, Athens was
spread out, quite distinct with its white houses and red roofs. On the

Pentelikon and mountains of Parnes snow had fallen! What a sight it was all round—but it was most beautiful towards the sea, which shone, so vast, so infinitely blue and dotted with white sails. The air was so transparent that I thought I could see the whole of the Peloponese.

As I walked down I met my traveling companion, the Persian from Herat. He nodded in familiar fashion, shook me by the hand and pointed out over the sea. It was our parting.

During my stay in Athens, in sunshine and rain, I visited the Acropolis daily. Here I celebrated my birthday with a visit, here I read my letters from home. The Acropolis was the last place in Athens that I visited before I left: it is on the Acropolis that my thoughts dwell the longest when they revisit Greece. . . .

A Rainy Day in Athens

Heavy rain clouds hung across the mountain of Hymettos: the weather was gray and cold. The unpaved streets stood in yellow mud from the rain during the night; the thin walls of the houses dripped with water. One of the country's most important people is the postman, a Greek, who rides with the letters and money overland to Patras. He arrived in his heavy wet sheepskin, leading his burdened horse, his loaded pistols hung round its neck, it was dragging its legs. They stopped at the apothecary's and the animal's sore legs were treated with ointment.

The rain was falling in large drops and soon there was a downpour. Three different flocks of sheep stood in the narrow square in front of the church; they huddled together, closer and closer. The shepherds leaned on their long staffs. Closely wrapped in thick brown smocks, with their shapeless hats pulled over their heads, they looked more like Greenlanders than what we think of as Greeks. They stood bare-legged in the mud. The rain poured down and eased off only towards evening, when the wind broke up the clouds and scattered them away like mist.

I ventured out. Creeping out from their low mud-huts were a couple of Negro families, who had been slaves under the Turks. The woman's entire costume consisted of a sort of gown and a soiled skirt. She lay and scooped out water over the doorstep, while small black children, one wearing nothing but a red wool shirt, danced in the mud.

The whole stretch from here, the last house in the street, and out to the Pentelikon and the mountains of Parnes seemed to be wild and without road or path. A man in a sheepskin coat, pipe in mouth, was riding over the heath; his wife and grown daughter ran behind. The wife was carrying a baby in a bag on her back; under one arm she had an iron cooking pot and under the other an empty pig-skin in which there had been wine. The daughter was dragging a large bundle. They were talking loudly and happily; the man turned round solemnly and nodded, rode more briskly and his wife and daughter held on by the tail so that they could keep up with him. Everything was in fine order—each person was, according to custom and habit, in his right place.

What a picture! These bare mountains, where the clouds hung wet and heavy as if they would crash down into the valley—and the valley itself, without huts, without the herdsman's fires, only with pale-gray thyme and this nomad family! Where the wide busy road used to go, where young, clever Athenians made their way to Plato's Academy, there now rides through the tall heath plants, dumb-witted, the poor wretched peasant. And the donkey knows which track to follow. The place which in the time of Plato became sacred, that place from which the light of the spirit streamed out over the rest of Europe, now produces only a huddle of stunted olive trees. The mound of rubbish nearby is Colonus, with which the immortal name of Oedipus is associated.

I took the way out there, over the wet heath. I stood on Colonus. . . . and the wind blew cold and sharp from the mountains, rain clouds chased past. . . .

The Rhapsodists

The Greeks have a kind of itinerant musician—the *rhapsodist*: they are usually old, blind men, each in his appearance a real Homer, but there are also younger lads who have chosen this way of life through inclination and musical talent. They know an incredible number of songs. By the watch-fires on the hills, by the hearths of the wealthy Greeks, they deliver their songs, producing complete pieces of music on the mandolins.

It was my intention, during the last days of March, to make an excursion to Delphi: I could have spent my birthday—April 2—on Parnassus, the real Parnassus, but the gods willed otherwise. The valleys around Delphi were covered with snow, the rivers had over-flowed their banks and it was raw and cold. I had to stay in Athens, but the Muses were favorable to me and on that day I got both song and music—the most special that I heard in Greece.

When I came down from the Acropolis, where I had spent part of the morning alone, I found on my table a letter with an invitation from Ross. Since I could not come that day to Parnassus, Parnassus would come to me! More one could not ask! Here at that moment had come to Athens two wandering *rhapsodists*, young Greeks from Smyrna, who were to sing the best folksongs for me. But we had to hear them indoors because it was still wet and stormy.

I went to Ross's house. the musicians took their places; they sat with the left leg over the right; one had his Venetian mandolin on his lap, the other played the violin, an instrument which had only recently been taken up by these wandering singers. Each wore Greek blue clothes and had a red fez on his head; both had pleasant lively faces, dark eyes and beautifully arched eyebrows.

I think it was by chance, but it was certainly very strange that in the order in which they sang their songs, they gave quite a new history of Greece.

60

They began with a Greek lament, composed by a people who were still under the Turkish yoke; they sang of their flocks and their daughters who were abducted. It did not sound as it usually does when two are singing one and the same song. No, the voices crossed and intertwined with each other in harmony, each had its sorrow, its loss, but it was yet the same story, the same suffering which was expressed. The tone was both gentle and lamenting, as if fear constrained their tongues; but sometimes the hurt and pain swelled up into a wild cry, as if the whole people wept. It was moving, it gripped the heart like the song of Israel by the waters of Babylon.

Then followed a song of Rhigas[1] and with much feeling and enthusiasm they sang the strophe:

"Sparta, Sparta, can you sleep?
Wake, awake from your deep sleep of death!"

And then there came a war song which in melody was akin to the *Marseillaise* and yet I was told, it was original Greek, describing the fight of the Greeks, and the musicians sang the verses that the people had sung on King Otto's entry into Nauplia.[2] I felt much moved—a people's history written in music goes much more deeply to the heart than that written in words.

Suddenly the youngest musician plucked at the strings of the violin and played a potpourri from *Fra Diavolo* and *Robert* and other French operas. It was dreadful! It suddenly came to me like a vision, how all the real folk tunes would be silenced and foreign songs would infiltrate into the people; already the Greeks would rather hear Auber-type tunes than their own songs.

---

[1] A famous song by Rhigas, (1757–98), a Greek poet and freedom martyr. Rhigas lived in Venice as a rich merchant and gave the whole of his fortune to the education of young Greeks. His songs, which are now on all lips, contributed much to the awakening of the oppressed people to thoughts of liberation. He was handed over by Austria to the Turks, who executed him in Belgrade. H.C.A.

[2] King Otto was only seventeen, the son of Louis I of Bavaria, when he was placed on the Greek throne in 1832 by a convention of Great Britain, France and Russia. He endeared himself to the Greeks by wearing Greek dress on his arrival at Nauplia, the first capital of Greek independence. But ten years of rule, in which his Bavarian ministers took the lead, brought about rebellion. A revolution in 1843 resulted in the granting of a constitution. In 1862 he was forced to abdicate and he went into exile in Bavaria where he died.

As a finale we had a Turkish song; I have never heard anything more awful! I thought at first that it was a parody, but Ross assured me that this was not the case and later, in Smyrna and Constantinople, I was convinced of the truth of this. One voice began, quite gentle and incomprehensible even to those who knew Turkish; the voice jangled as if a dreamer were muttering something. I seemed to be hearing a drunken opium-eater moaning in a hideous dream. The accompaniment consisted entirely of strumming on one and the same string, always on the same note. There was something fearfully and inwardly despairing in this song and the refrain sounded as if the singer had suddenly awakened and screamed because he was being murdered.

When the musicians left us they each seized our hands, kissed them and, in the Greek custom, laid them on their foreheads.

In the morning Greek songs, in the evening folk dances—it was a real "Festival day." Lüth, the Queen's court chaplain, arranged for me to see this sight. The dancers were simple people—his two Greek servants, an old waiter from a coffee-house and then two young apprentices from the city. The musicians let the mandolin and the violin sing out and now and then one of them sang a short sentence or a challenge or an appeal for happiness—"Rejoice!," "Life is short!," "Love is sorrow, love is joy!," "Come, dance all you young ones!"

They all moved gracefully over the floor. The one on the outside acted as a kind of dancing choir-leader; the others watched his steps and posture, which they then copied. The nursemaid in the house, a Greek from Zea, who was very lovely, had put on her best clothes; the turban was especially decorative with her dark hair and beautiful forehead. She began, with two of the men, a dance from her native district. One could not have wished for anything more charming and yet, as I have said, all the dancers were simple people. She did not hold the men's hands, but clasped their belts; they touched the upper part of her arms and slowly they moved backwards and forwards, as though walking. All her movements spoke of peace; the men on the other hand breathed life and passion—she would try to break away from them, they held her fast, her eyes and face expressed strong emotions, but only one of the men was favored.

After they had danced and sung for us, two of the guests performed a Tyrolean dance for them. This seemed to appeal to them very much, and during the dance they copied the various movements. One of the musicians who, it was said, had some poetic talent, asked if they might hear a song from the North, "a hyperborean song" as he put it.

I told him about the song of the Danish peasant who asked if he could bear the body of King Frederik to its last resting place.[3] And he heard how the people sang a deep sorrowful Farewell from the ramparts of the city. And how the coffin was carried by torchlight along the snow-covered highway, a poor light was lit in the smallest hut by the wayside and there stood the old folk with their grandchildren; they saw the torches burning, folded their hands and said, "Now comes the King's body!" And as I sang this song I saw tears in the nursemaid's eyes. When I had finished the youngest of the musicians asked to hear the words again.

"He must have been a good king," he said and with a pleading look, he asked me to repeat the melody, and I sang it again.

When I left, late in the evening, the two musicians went with me. It was no longer raining, but over the heavens the mist clouds were passing, light and transparent so that one could see the stars twinkling through them. The great silent plain stretched out by our side towards the high mountains. It was as still as at night in the Cathedral of Roskilde, where King Frederik rests.

Suddenly, one of the musicians grabbed his violin and played some phrases of the melody to *The Danish Peasant and King Frederik*—perhaps he will compose some verses himself after what he had heard, and, between the Greek mountains and under the shady plane trees of Asia, he will sing a song about the King in the Northern land who was borne to his grave by the sorrowing peasant.

---

[3] *Lament Over Frederik VI* was a song cantata with words by Hans C. Andersen and music by J. P. E. Hartmann (1805–1900), a well-known Danish composer. Frederik VI died in 1839.

Daphne

Halfway between Athens and Eleusis there lies in wild solitude the monastery of Daphne, ruined during the Revolution; it was built in Moorish style and is now used as a resting place for the gendarmes who patrol the roads. The church is 600 to 800 years old and is built on the site of a temple of Apollo. A great marble column is still found in the church walls; there were formerly three, but two of them have been taken away to England.

Undoubtedly Daphne is one of the most interesting and picturesque places between Athens and Eleusis: I was there with Ross and a Greek, Professor Philippos Ioannou.

We went into the cloisters which were overgown by tall nettles hiding open wells without any covers. We had to look out for them, step by step, in order not to fall in. Thus we came to the opposite wall, where it seemed the easiest to walk, and we soon found ourselves on the half fallen roof of the church; here the vegetation was as rich as the building was ruined. One step was the overturned top of an ancient marble sarcophagus, another step was the remains of a fluted porphyry pillar. Everywhere were thistles, mignonette and bird-grass. Bats flew over us in the broad daylight; here was their home, here their kingdom, even though the sun was shining on their wings.

Inside the monastery itself the monks' cells have been converted into a vast stable, in which the gendarmes have their horses; they neigh where the monks once prayed.

The church is magnificent and could still be restored. We stood under the cupola which is decorated with an ornate picture of Christ. In His left hand the Saviour holds a bible; His right hand is stretched out in blessing. During the Revolution the Turks encamped here and lit fires in the church; the walls are still blackened by the smoke. They smoked their pipes and amused themselves by shooting at the Redeemer of the Christians up there in the dome, and their bullets hit one eye, His mouth and His halo—the marks are still clearly seen in the mosaic. They defaced the pictures of the saints—the icons—on the altar, drawing obscene pictures, while their companions laughed and shouted applause. A collection of skulls and bones, found under the bushes and nettles outside now lay thrown together in a corner between the altar itself and the high altar screen; typical of the Greek church, it has three apses and is painted from top to bottom with murals. These too had been defaced by the Turks, but three small lamps had been hung up and were burning. They are looked after by an old Greek who lives out in the woodshed and there makes coffee and pours a glass of *raki* for visitors. In this church he was baptized, in this church he made his pact of friendship, and here he was married.

Easter Celebrations in Greece

The Catholic Easter in Italy, especially in Rome, is wonderful, fascinating! It is an uplifting sight on the vast square of St. Peter's to see the whole throng of people sink to their knees and receive the Blessing. The Easter Festival in poor Greece cannot be celebrated with such splendor. But having seen both, one comes to the conclusion that in Rome it is a festival which, in its splendor and glory, comes out of the Church to the people; whereas in Greece it is a festival which flows out from the hearts and minds of the people—from their whole way of life—and the Church is only one link, one strand. Before Easter there is a long and rigorous fast, which is very strictly kept; the peasants virtually live only on bread, garlic and water.

The Athens newspaper came out on Good Friday with black edges because of the death of Christ: the little "vignette" showed a sarcophagus with a weeping willow and over it was a poem on the Passion. The festival itself began that evening. I went to the main church, which was beautifully lit up and filled to overflowing. Before the altar there was a coffin of glass panels, joined together with silver plates. The coffin was filled with fresh roses, which were intended to represent the dead Christ. A remarkable buzzing from the praying congregation echoed through this House of God. The ornately vested priests and Bishops came and went before the altar, where they read their prayers. At nine o'clock in the evening there was the sound of mourning music and the procession began from the church through the main street to the palace. The slow-moving procession was one of the most impressive I have ever witnessed. It was a wonderful star-clear evening, so mild and calm; all around on every balcony and by the open windows, stood onlookers, each with a lighted candle in hand. Music sounded from the side streets; the smell and smoke of incense filled the air. A great throng of people moved forward, each and every one in his best clothes, each—even the smallest child—with a long thin burning

Greeks in native costumes.

candle in hand. The funeral music of the military bands sounded as though the people were bearing their King to his grave. Surrounded by priests, the coffin was borne with the fresh red roses; over it hung a long mourning-band, held by the chief officials of the country and high-ranking officers. A crowd of these and then the vast throng of the ordinary people completed the procession. There was a quiet, an apparent sadness, sorrow and devotion which could not but grip everyone present. Outside the palace, where the King and Queen were standing, the Bishop preached a short sermon and the King kissed the Holy Bible. During the whole ceremony the church bells rang—always just twice on the same note and then a short pause. Night and day the church was filled with people and at midnight before Easter Day the King and Queen and the whole court were there; the priests stood praying and mourning around the flower-filled coffin and everyone prayed quietly. The clock struck twelve and at that very moment the Bishop stepped forward and proclaimed, "Christ is risen!"

"Christ is risen!" shouted everyone with jubilation! Kettledrums and trumpets sounded; the band played a joyful dance tune. People fell on each others' necks, kissed and rejoiced: "Christ is risen!" Outside the sound of cannon was heard, rockets flared into the air and bonfires were lit. Men and boys, each with candle in hand, danced in a long row through the town. The women lit fires, killed lamb and roasted it in the street. Small children, who had all received new red shoes and a new fez danced just in their shirts round the fire, kissed each other and said, like their elders, "Christ is risen." I could have pressed each one of these children to my heart and rejoiced with the "Christ is risen!": it was moving, uplifting and beautiful!

It may be said that the whole thing was just ceremony and further— and certainly with some truth—that this was natural human gladness that the rigorous fast was over, and that they now could eat their lamb and drink their wine was what made them so happy. Very well— let us make some allowance for this, but I dare believe and I will say that here was something more. Here there was a true religious rejoicing. Christ was in their thoughts as on their lips: "Christ is risen!" sounded the tidings and it was not an ancient happening, no, it was as if it had taken place that night, in their land. It was as if the news of this had just at that moment reached their ears!

The Court in Athens

It was from the olive grove, on the way from Eleusis, that King Otto saw for the first time the Acropolis and his royal capital, Athens, which at that time was little better than a rubbish heap with some wretched mud huts and a few half-timbered buildings. A couple of these, attached to a kind of garden section, became his temporary palace until the new marble residence is completed.

It is a very modest building in which the King lives—anywhere else in Europe it would serve for a private person's summer villa. There is a path of grass with a few bushes as decoration in front, and every day the main guard musters here to music from *La Muette de Portici*, *Scaramouche* and *L'Elisir d'amore*. The Greek nursemaids jig the babies up and down to the cheerful tunes.

The young and very lovable Queen was brought up in her native Oldenborg in modest circumstances; she was content to move into this poor palace here and the people greeted her with joy and gladness. I was told that, at her coming, all the streets were strewn with roses: she herself was, on the other hand, to have a bouquet of rarer and also more beautiful flowers. Potatoes had just recently been introduced into Greece and people were feeling the benefit of them; the flower of the potato plant seemed to the Greeks to be the rarest and loveliest flower and so they offered the Queen who came to them from Oldenborg a bouquet of potato flowers.

How much the King and Queen have given up to live here; how many sorrows, for the sake of this land and people, pierce the King's heart, the King who is alone in a ruined, classical land, rich in great memories. He is alone among a people—yes, I know them too little to judge, but I do not love this race; the Turks on the other hand pleased me much more; they were honorable and good-natured.

Each year the King and Queen make a tour of the country. Everywhere they are received with jubilation. People come long distances with their complaints and petitions; the young King hears them all, has every case investigated and these journeys often bring much good. But they are not in themselves very comfortable although everything is done to lessen the difficulties which any journey in Greece involves. Servants are sent on ahead, tents are put up where the party can stay overnight; tables are set up in the wild hills, the champagne corks pop and shepherds and shepherdesses dance on the plain outside the tent while the evening sun shines on the solitary marble column and the high mountains. It is a natural decoration and a ballet which only the classical scene, where the real gods once trod, can offer. But there often is considerable discomfort to be met with and there are very unpleasant and painful moments. Last year in a small village, the day before the royal tour arrived, fourteen robbers had been there. When the King heard this news he immediately went in pursuit with the whole of his small bodyguard. The Queen with her ladies and some gentlemen stayed behind, anxiously awaiting the outcome. The King, however, found none of the robbers. But some of the local farmers were more fortunate and they captured several the following night, gave them a short trial, cut their heads off and with these came running in the early morning to the royal tent.

Up to that time the King had signed only one sentence of death, and that was on a well-known and abominable brigand. The Greeks who would not themselves hesitate to behead such a villain, could not, however, understand that the law of the land could allow this penalty, and they demonstrated this last year. The Government was forced to get an executioner from Malta because no Greek would take on the job.

The brigand, led by the guard and a vast throng of people, was taken out to the olive grove, but when he got there and the German soldiers had made a circle around him, he protested against the execution; "It is something we are not used to here!" he said and began to fight with the executioner. It must have been a dreadful sight—the fight lasted nearly two hours and the soldiers dared not intervene. "We must take care that he does not escape," they said. "That is our duty." It came to the point when the executioner was very nearly beheaded by the brigand but, exhausted and wounded, the latter at last sank down to the ground, where he received the death blow. The executioner was said later to have been secretly murdered. I tell this story simply as it was told to me in Athens.

The Pact of Friendship (A STORY)

In my small sketches I have tried to depict a little part of Athens and its surroundings, and I know how colorless the picture is that I have given; what an inadequate impression it is of Greece, this sorrowing, mourning Genius of Beauty, whose grandeur and sorrow the stranger never forgets.

Perhaps better than I with my pictures, the solitary shepherd up in the wild mountains can open your eyes with a simple story of one of the events of his life. Let him speak, says my Muse! Very well—the shepherd here on the mountain shall tell us about a custom, a beautiful, unique and old custom—the Pact of Friendship.[1]

The walls of our home were made of mud, but the door was framed by grooved marble pillars, which had been found there when the house was built. The roof almost touched the ground; it was now dark and ugly but when it was made the oleanders and fresh laurel branches, brought from the other side of the mountains, were fresh and flowering. There was only a narrow plot of land around our house; behind, rock walls rose steeply, bare and dark. Often they were covered by clouds that looked like living white figures. Never have I heard a bird sing there, never did the men here dance to the tune of the bagpipes; but the place was sacred from ancient times—it is called Delphi! The dark brooding mountains lie covered with snow; the highest, on which the evening sun shines longest, is Parnassus. The stream that runs past our house comes down from there; it too was once sacred but now the mule muddies it with his feet, although the current is so swift that the water is soon clear again. How I remember it all and its holy, deep loneliness! The fire was lit in the middle of the hut and when the hot ashes were piled high and glowing, the bread was baked inside.

---

[1] *The Pact of Friendship* is included in Andersen's collected stories.

When the snow lay so high round the hut that it was almost hidden, then my mother seemed the happiest—she would hold my head between her hands, kiss my forehead and sing the songs that she otherwise never sang—because the Turks, our masters, forbade their singing.

On the top of Mount Olympus, among the low fir trees, sat an old stag; its eyes were heavy with tears; red, green and pale blue tears he shed and a young buck came by and said: "What is wrong with you that you are weeping and shedding red, green and even pale blue tears?" "The Turk has come to our city, he has wild hounds for the chase, a mighty pack!" "I will chase them over the island," said the buck "and into the deep sea!" But before evening the stag was killed, and before nightfall the hart was hunted and dead. . . .

And when my mother sang this song, her eyes were wet and there was a tear in her long lashes—but she hid it and turned the black bread in the ashes. Then I shook my fist and said, "We will kill the Turk!"—but she repeated the end of the song; "I will chase them over the islands into the deep sea"—but before evening the stag was killed and before nightfall the hart was hunted and dead.

For some nights and days we had been alone in the hut and then my father came. I knew he might bring me mussel-shells from the Bay of Lepanto or perhaps even a knife, sharp and shining. But this time he brought us a child, a little naked girl, whom he was carrying under his sheepskin cloak; she was wrapped in a sheepskin and all she had when she was freed from this on my mother's lap were three silver coins bound into her black hair.

Father told us about the Turks who had killed the child's parents; he told us so much that I dreamed about it all night. My father was himself wounded; mother bandaged his arm, the wound was deep and his thick sheepskin was frozen stiff with blood.

The little girl was to be my sister—she was lovely; my mother's eyes were not clearer and kinder than hers! Anastasia, as she was called, was to be my sister because her father was bound to my father according to an old custom which we still maintain. In their youth they had sworn a vow of brotherhood, choosing the most beautiful and virtuous girl in the neighborhood to unite them in this Pact of Friendship. I heard often about this beautiful and special custom.

Now the little one had become my sister; she sat on my lap, I brought her flowers and feathers from the mountain birds; we drank together of the water of Parnassus, we slept cheek by cheek under the laurel-leaf roof of the hut. But for many winters yet my mother sang of the red, green and pale blue tears—and I did not yet understand that it was my own people whose thousandfold sorrows were mirrored in those tears. . . .

One day there came strangers, whose clothes were different from ours. They had their beds and tents with them on pack-horses and more than twenty Turks, all with sword and pistol, escorted them, because they were friends of the Pasha and had letters from him. They came only to see our mountains, in snow and cloud to climb Parnassus and to see the unique, dark steep rocks around our hut. They could not in any case endure the smoke which drifted up to the ceiling and out through the low door, so they pitched their tents out on the narrow plot near the hut and roasted lamb and birds and poured sweet strong wine—which the Turks do not drink.

When they left I followed them for part of the way, carrying my little sister Anastasia on my back in a goatskin bag. One of the foreign gentlemen stood me against a rock and sketched the two of us—so life-like as we stood there, we looked like one being. Never had I thought about it, but Anastasia and I were indeed like one; always she lay in my lap or on my back and if I dreamed she was in my dreams.

Two nights later some other people came to our hut; they were armed with knives and pistols. They were Albanians—bold folk as my mother said. They were there only a short time; my sister Anastasia sat on the lap of one of them—and when he was gone she had two, not three, silver coins in her hair. They rolled tobacco in long strips of paper and smoked it. The oldest talked about the way they should go and was uncertain about it. "If I spit upwards," he said, "it falls on my face and if I spit downwards, it falls into my beard!" But one way or another they had to choose. They went and my father followed them and shortly afterwards we heard shots and then again. And then soldiers came to our hut and took my mother, Anastasia and me. They said that robbers had stayed with us and that my father had joined up with them, and so we must leave. I saw the bodies of the robbers. I saw my father's body and I wept until I fell asleep. When I woke up we were in prison, but the cell was not more wretched than the room in our own hut and I was given onion and resinated wine which they poured from a tarred sack—and better we did not have at home.

How long we were prisoners I do not know, but many nights and days went by. When we were let out it was our holy Festival of Easter. I carried Anastasia on my back, because my mother was ill; she could walk only slowly and it was a long time before we reached the sea. It was the Bay of Lepanto. We went into a church which shone with pictures on a background of gold; they were angels and so beautiful— but all the same I thought that our little Anastasia was just as beautiful. In the middle of the floor stood a coffin filled with roses; my mother said it was the Saviour Christ who lay there. And the priest proclaimed, "Christ is risen!" and all the people kissed each other. Everyone held a lighted candle in his hand; even I had one and so did little Anastasia. The bagpipes sounded, the men danced hand in hand from the church and outside the women roasted the Easter lamb. We were invited; I sat by the fire and a boy, older than I, put his arm around me, kissed me and said, "Christ is risen!"—and so for the first time we met, we two, Aphtanides and I.

My mother knew how to make fish nets; by the Bay this gave her a good income and we stayed a long time by the sea—the lovely sea which tasted like tears and in its colors reminded me of the tears of the stag; sometimes they were red, sometimes green and then soon after, blue again.

Aphtanides knew how to steer a boat and I sat with my little sister Anastasia in the boat which skimmed over the water as a cloud floats in the air. When the sun went down the mountains looked darker blue than ever—one range peeped over another and farthest away stood Parnassus, topped with snow. In the evening sun the peak shone like glowing iron; it looked as if the light came from within the mountain, because it shone far in the blue, glistening light, long after the sun had gone down. White sea-birds flapped their wings, mirrored in the clear water, otherwise it was as still here as at Delphi between the dark mountains. I lay on my back in the boat, Anastasia sat on my chest and the stars above gleamed ever brighter than the lamps in our church. They were the same stars and they stood in the same place over me as when I sat outside our hut near Delphi. At last I dreamed I was still there! There was a splash and the boat rocked violently—I screamed because Anastasia had fallen into the water. But Aphtanides was quick and handed her up to me! We took her clothes off and wrung the water out and then dressed her again. Aphtanides and I did the same with ours and we stayed out until they were dry again—and no one knew the fright we had had for my little foster-sister, whose life Aphtanides now had a part in.

It was summer. The sun was so hot that the trees withered; I thought of our cool mountains and the fresh water up there. My mother too longed for home and one evening we made our way back there. How silent and still it was! We walked over the wild thyme which was still scented even though the sun had dried its leaves. We met not one shepherd, passed not one hut. Everything was still and lonely; only a shooting star said that there was life up there in the heavens. I do not know whether the light came from the air itself or from the twinkling stars, but we could clearly see the outline of all the mountains. My mother lit a fire and cooked the onions she had brought with her and I and my little sister slept in the thyme without fear of the hideous smidraki,[2] from whose mouth comes flame, or of the wolves and jackals. My mother was sitting close beside us and I believed that this was protection enough.

We reached our old home, but the hut was a heap of rubble and we had to rebuild it. A couple of women helped my mother and in a few days the walls were up and a new roof of oleander had been laid over them. Mother plaited covers of skin and bark for wine bottles;

---

[2] Greek superstition says that this monster comes from the stomach of a slaughtered sheep which is strewn on the fields.

I looked after the priests' little herd;[3] Anastasia and the little tortoises were my playmates.

One day we had a visit from our dear Aphtanides; he longed so much to see us he said, and he stayed for two whole days.

After a month he came again and told us that he was going by ship to Patras and Corfu, but he had first to say goodbye to us. He brought a big fish for my mother. He had so much to tell us, not only about the fishermen down in the Bay of Lepanto, but also about the kings and heroes who had once ruled in Greece as the Turks do now.

I have seen a rosebush in bud and in days and weeks the bud becomes a flower in full bloom—I have seen this happen without thinking about it and, before I realized it, how big, lovely and blushing it was. This is what happened to me as regards Anastasia. She was a beautiful, grown girl—I, a sturdy youth. The wolf skins on my mother's and Anastasia's bed I had myself stripped from the animals which had fallen to my gun. Years had gone by. . . .

One evening Aphtanides arrived, slim as a reed, strong and sun-tanned. He kissed us all, and told us about the mighty ocean, about Malta's fortress and the pyramids of Egypt. It sounded extraordinary—like one of the priest's legends. I looked up to him with new respect.

"How much you know," I said, "and how well you tell a story!"

"But you once told me the most beautiful story," he said. "You told me, and I have never forgotten it, about the beautiful old custom of the Pact of Friendship—a custom I would dearly love to follow! My brother, as your father and Anastasia's father did, let us two go to church—the fairest and most virtuous maiden is your sister, Anastasia; she shall unite us. No one has a more beautiful custom than we Greeks!"

Anastasia blushed, like a fresh rose. My mother kissed Aphtanides.

The little church was about an hour's walk from our hut, where there was a little soil and a few trees were able to grow. A silver lamp hung in front of the altar.

I had on my best clothes; my white *fustanella* fitted well over my

---

[3] A farmer who can read often becomes a priest and is called "Holy Father"; people kiss the ground when they meet him. HCA.

hips, my red jacket sat narrow and tight and there was silver in the tassel of my fez; in my belt were my knife and pistol. Aphtanides was wearing the blue costume of the Greek sailors, a silver medallion of the Virgin Mary hung round his neck, his scarf was costly as only rich men could afford; everyone could see that we were going to something special. We went into the little lonely church, where the evening sun shone through the door on to the lighted lamp and the mosaic pictures on their golden ground. We kneeled on the altar steps and Anastasia stood in front of us. She was wearing a white dress that hung loose and light over her lovely body; her white neck and breast were covered by a chain of old and new coins, linked together and forming a complete collar. Her black hair was piled up on her head in a single coil, held in place by a little cap of silver and gold coins found in one of the ancient temples—no Greek girl could have finer jewels. Her face was radiant, her eyes were like stars.

All three of us silently said our prayers. Then she asked us, "Will you be friends in life and death?" We answered, "Yes." "Will you both remember that, whatever happens, your brother is a part of you, your secret is his, your happiness is his! Sacrifice, endurance, every-thing as for your own soul shall you bear for him?" And we repeated our "Yes." And she joined our hands together, kissed us on the forehead and we prayed again, in silence.

The priest came forth from behind the altar, blessed the three of us and the other priests sang an anthem. When we left I saw that my mother, standing by the church door, was weeping, much moved.

How happy we were in our little hut near the springs of Delphi!

The evening before Aphtanides had to leave, he and I sat, deep in thought, on the hillside; his arm was around my waist, mine was around his shoulders. We spoke of the plight of Greece, of the men who could be trusted; no thought did either of us hide from the other—and so I seized his hand and said:

"One more thing you must know which, up to this moment only God and I know: my soul is filled with love, a love stronger than that I have for my mother and for you."

"And whom do you love?" asked Aphtanides, and a deep flush spread over his face and neck.

"I love Anastasia," I said—and his hand trembled in mine and he became deathly pale; I saw it, and I understood! And I think that my hand shook too. I bent my head towards him, kissed his forehead and whispered, "I have never said a word to her—perhaps she does not love me!—My brother, remember that I have seen her every day, she has grown up by my side, she has grown into my soul."

"And she shall be yours," he said. "Yours—I cannot lie to you and will not do so! I love her too, but tomorrow I am going away: we shall meet again in a year, by which time you will be married of course! I have some money—it is yours! You must take it—you shall take it!" And slowly we walked over the mountains. It was late in the evening when we stood by my mother's hut.

Anastasia was holding the lamp when we walked inside; my mother was not there. Anastasia looked at Aphtanides with a curiously sorrowful expression. "Tomorrow you are leaving us," she said, "how sorry I shall be!"

"*You* will be sorry?" he said, and I felt that there was a hurt, a sadness in his words, as great as my own. "Your brother here loves you—do you love him? His love is as great as his silence!" And Anastasia trembled and burst into tears. I saw only her, thought only of her; I put my arm around her waist and said, "Yes, I love you!"

She put her lips to mine, her hands around my neck. The lamp had fallen to the ground—it was as dark around us as in the heart of dear, unhappy Aphtanides. . . .

Before daylight, he arose, kissed us all goodbye and left. His money he gave to my mother to keep for us.

A few days later Anastasia became my wife.

Departure From Greece

April 20, 1841

I was looking forward to so much that was new, great and unknown and yet I was very sad to leave Greece, where everything had elevated my thoughts from the littleness of everyday life, and every bitterness from home had been wiped out of my soul. . . .

In mid-morning I left Athens and drove to Piraeus, although the French steamship *Eurotas*, on which I had booked a berth, was not scheduled to leave before the evening. In Piraeus I met most of my friends from Athens: Pastor Lüth had his small children with him— they held out their hands to me, and the Greek servants seized my hand and, nodding happily, wished me well. On board Ross was the last Dane I saw. He pressed me to his heart—it was a sad moment for me. "I shall come back to Greece" I said, as if to reassure myself— may they be prophetic words!

I was now alone. From the shore the ladies were waving their handkerchiefs; every goodbye had been said. I was handed a letter of recommendation from Prokesch-Osten[1] to the Baron Stürmer, the Austrian Inter-Nuncius in Constantinople and a very influential man. Prokesch-Osten had himself gone that morning to Thebes; his intelligent and attractive wife sent me a short note of farewell and inside there was a copy of Prokesch's magnificent poem *Gebet in der Wüste*.

When he had gone I had only Greeks, Armenians and Asiatic Jews for company—apart from the ship's crew. We were due to sail at sunset. I was affected—the sea was running high. I wanted to sleep the whole way to Syra just as I had previously done from Syra to Piraeus. I lay down in my cabin and slept. It was only when they weighed anchor

---

[1] Anton Prokesch-Osten (1795–1876) was the Austrian Minister in Athens from 1834 to 1849. Andersen met him in Greece, and again in Germany in 1855. The section of this book about Greece is dedicated to Prokesch-Osten, and a poem called *Den Sabel Sur Seite, Geschoss in der Hand* by Prokesch-Osten is given in full in the original of Andersen's German edition.

and I heard the noise that I woke up. There was no movement in the sea and quickly I put my coat on and ran up on deck in order to see the town of Syros. But when I got there I saw—Piraeus, the mount of Hymettos and Parnes. We would leave only in the early morning; the Captain had waited for royal dispatches and these had only now arrived. It was 4 o'clock in the morning.

We sailed in fairly smooth waters; the sun rose and with every hour shone the more strongly. One large umbrella after another was put up. The passengers formed very picturesque groups. On a gun emplacement sat a Greek woman, feeding her baby; an older girl, poor but attractive and very clean, stood leaning against the cannon. The men smoked cigarettes and admired an Arab's damascene sword. Someone asked me if I was a Bavarian and when I said that I was Danish I was again greeted as American.

In the strong sunlight the marble columns of the Temple at Cape Kolones—the ruins of Sunium—stood out, white and shining; sea birds wheeled around the gray, deserted coast.

Zea was stretched out before us and soon we saw Syros with its bare rock face. We had to go right around the island to reach the harbor. Here I had been before, here I was no longer a stranger.

The steamship on which I was to go to Constantinople had not yet arrived. I went to the *Hotel della Grece* and not an hour later the landlord told me that Greek soldiers had arrived to take me to the townhall—the authorities wanted to talk to me! What could they want? I went with two guards and came into a dark horrible building, where a Greek official asked me in a sharp voice and in bad Italian if I had a passport. I produced mine, he read and read, but the passport, issued in Copenhagen, was written in French and Danish and he understood neither of these languages.

"There is a German whom we should arrest and send back to Athens," said the man; "I do not understand a word of your passport, but I believe you are German and the man we are looking for, and so you must go back to Athens!"

I tried to explain the contents of my passport to him, but he would not understand me. "Very well," I said and took out the letter of introduction I had received in Athens to the Greek Minister in Constantinople, Christides, the former Governor on Syros—to whom I was, in the best possible terms, recommended, "Be good enough to read who I am." The man took the letter and immediately became courtesy itself. He made many excuses and I was escorted back to my hotel with great civility. And there I met again the Russian who had been robbed on his journey from Constantinople—still just as angry as before and cursing the Orient and all the poets who aroused a desire in others to go there. . . .

Part Three
THE ORIENT

A Storm in the Archipelago

Early in the morning I was rowed out from the harbor of Syra to the French steamship *Rhamses* which had come from Marseilles and had had a very stormy passage. The weather had not yet completely settled itself down. The wind whistled in the rigging, and the waves broke over the side of the ship.

There were shouting and screams from Greek and Jewish women who were traveling to Smyrna. Before they were allowed on board each of them had to show their tickets—which were hidden in a knot in a shawl or scarf that could not be loosened, or they had been given to a relative in another boat. They were all dreadfully upset and anxious, and the sailor who was guarding the gangway barred with his halberd each one who did not immediately produce a ticket. One fat Greek woman bellowed very loudly indeed.

The poor wretched deck passengers were herded together in the part of the ship assigned to them and a guard was put over them. Discipline seemed to be very strict on the steamship *Rhamses*. (In Athens I heard only two French ships praised as comfortable for all passengers—and they were the *Leonidas* and the *Lycurgus* on which I had previously sailed.)

We sailed right in under the coast of Tenos, which looked well inhabited and fertile. Villages lay close together. One of them was a fair size with a pretty church, and was surrounded by vineyards and cultivated fields. Three ranges of hills rose, one behind the other. We sailed so near to the rock face that I thought we could feel the surge breaking on the ship. The sea rose higher and higher; it was as if the storm came out of the hills on Tenos. The open sea lay before us— foam white and black! Waves were already breaking over the ship. The wretched deck passengers huddled up by the funnel, getting nearer and nearer to it. No one stopped them now since all the sailors had

85

something else to do. The sail was hoisted but immediately brought down again. The captain's pipe shrilled, there was shouting, noise, wailing and sea-sickness—all increasing by the minute. I was still on deck although several times the ship slid down into the trough of great long waves. The Greek women clung to each other and howled. On the deck children lay as though half dead, and the sea smashed over the ship so that everyone was soaked. And under all this we were ringed around by sea-gulls, looking like the winged hour-glass of invisible Death. Every timber in the ship creaked and we went from the stars down into the deep—and then up again to the stars.

In the end I went to my cabin. Everything rattled, everything creaked. I heard the mate's pipe, the officers' commands, the shutters being closed, masts cracking, the waves smiting the ship so that it stood still with every timber groaning. Near to me someone called on the Madonna and all the Saints! Another cursed. I was convinced that we should perish and when I quite clearly thought and accepted this I felt much calmer. My thoughts were with all my dear ones in Denmark. "How much has been done for me and how little have I achieved!" That was the sorrow that weighed on my heart. I thought of my friends: God bless them and make them happy, was my silent prayer. "Let me in another world do what I have not done here. Everything of value in me was Yours. Everything You have given me— Your will be done!" And I closed my eyes. The storm whistled over the sea, the ship shook, like a sparrow in a whirlwind, but I slept, slept from physical exhaustion—and with the intercession of a good angel.

When I awoke, I could still hear the waves breaking against the ship, but the vessel was gliding calmly, like a swan gently rocking on the water. We were in shelter, in the lee of the bay of Smyrna and I, like all the Greek ladies, had certainly expected to awaken in another world—and yet in fact this had happened. I stood on deck and before me lay another world—the coast of Asia.

Smyrna

April 23, 1841

The sea in the wide deep bay of Smyrna looked yellow-green like a quarantine flag. The coast of Asia reminded me of Sicily, but it was much more fertile. The sun was burning hot. I looked at the part of the world at the sight of which Moses from Egypt had marveled, that part of the world where Christ was born, had taught and had suffered. I saw the coast from which Homer's song had sounded over the earth. I should now set foot in the Orient.

We passed a fort; the coast to the right was covered with olive groves, in the middle of which lay a large village with red-brown houses, flowering fruit trees and a fresh greensward. Beyond the olive grove there was a natural park with leafy trees and high cypresses. Straight in front of us lay Smyrna.

Most of the houses were brown, their roofs red and pointed as in the North. At the side of almost every house an uncountable number of cypress trees had been planted; they were as high as our poplars. Slender white minarets, the first I had seen, rose above the tall dark cypresses. In the eastern quarters of the town, down towards the bay where the foreign consuls live, flags of all nations hung on high poles. Behind the town there rose a green hill with a little cypress wood surmounted by the remains of a ruined fort.

The harbor was crowded with shipping; there were several steamships, including one Turkish vessel, flying the red flag with the crescent. A boat filled with veiled Turkish women was heading for the steamer. These white mummified figures reminded me of funeral processions in Rome.

We cast anchor. I set foot on land.

It was foretold at my cradle that I should visit the coast of Asia. My thoughts were full of great memories and the first thing my eyes fell on was a theater poster. A French company was here and that evening was playing *La Reine de seize ans*[1] and *Les premiers amours*. Queen Christina of Sweden was very fond of flaunting herself—but she surely could never have dreamed that she would be on show in a theater in Asia before an audience of Greeks and Turks.

I went into the nearest street—one would call it an alley-way at home. A mass of small dark streets ran into it. From his window one neighbor could comfortably take a pinch of his neighbor's snuff! The houses are half-timbered or simply of wood, not very high and in the main street, where I was, most of the ground floor rooms were open shops with all sorts of goods. This main street wound at an angle through the length of the town and ended in the higher part with the Bazaar.

It is said that, in order to avoid the plague, one must never come into contact with other people, but this is an impossibility in the main street of Smyrna; it is too narrow and too crowded. I met whole flocks of women swathed in long muslin veils, so that only the tip of the nose and their dark eyes were visible. There were Armenians in long blue and black gowns with large black hats shaped like up-turned stew-pots on their shaved heads, there were fancily dressed Greeks, dirty Jews, and grave Turks with their hookahs being carried in front of them by a boy. High up on the hump of a camel there was a kind of *calash* or carriage with colored curtains, through which a veiled female head peered out. A Bedouin with bare legs, his head almost hidden in his white burnoose like a mummified lion, went with quick steps through the throng.

I met a half-naked black boy driving two large ostriches in front of him with a stick. Each of them looked like a worn out trunk on stilts, to which stuck a bloody swan's neck. They were two ugly creatures—but they added to the picturesque scene. From some shops the scent of musk and myrrh wafted out. Costumes from three quarters of the

---

[1] *La Reine de 16 Ans* was a popular play by J. F. A. Bayard (1796–1853) about Queen Christina of Sweden (1626–89). HCA translated it—probably from the German version by Theodor Hell—and it was in the Danish repertory for many years after its first production at the Royal Theatre in Copenhagen on 29 March 1833.

globe made up a motley sight. And there was a medley of languages—Arabic, Turkish, Greek, Italian.

In the middle of the crowd my guide pointed to a gentlemen in Western dress and said, "That is the Danish Consul, Herr Jongh." I introduced myself to him as a Dane and soon we were walking arm in arm through the long street. By chance I had at once met in Smyrna the one person to whom, as a Dane, I could best turn. Herr Jongh was, however, just about to go to Constantinople with one of the Turkish steamers, (whose speed he praised)—but we would meet again in Pera.

On the outskirts of the town, where the road seemed to be leading into the interior of the country, there was a Turkish *khan*. In front of it lay large cushions and straw mats and on these a number of Turks in colored caftans and turbans reclined smoking their pipes. Large open wagons were drawn by white oxen which were hung about with metal plaques, red braids and tassels. One wagon, driven by a fat old Turk, was quite full of veiled women sitting in a clump on the bottom of the cart. I am sure they were beautiful! For behind many a grill in every street there must have been a collection of houris, but they were, as a Turkish poet says, "hidden like rubies in a jewel-box, like rose-oil in the flask and like a parrot in a cage!"

A Rose from Homer's Grave (A STORY)

In all the songs of the Orient there is an echo of the nightingale's love for the rose. In the silent star-clear nights, the winged songster offers a serenade to his fragrant flower.

Not far from Smyrna, under the tall plane trees the merchants rest their laden camels, which proudly stretch their long necks and clumsily tread the ground which is sacred. Here I saw a flowering rose hedge; wild doves flew among the branches of the trees high above, their wings shining in the sunlight like mother-of-pearl.

On the bush there was one rose, among all the flowers the most beautiful and to this one the nightingale sang out the sadness of love—but the rose was silent, not even a single dewdrop lay, like a tear of pity, on its petals: it bowed its head with its branch over some large stones.

"Here rests the world's greatest singer," said the rose, "my perfume shall scent the air over his grave and on it I will strew my petals when the storm tears them apart. The Singer of the *Iliad* became earth—in this earth from which I am sprung; I, a rose from Homer's grave, I am too sacred to blossom for a poor nightingale."

And the nightingale sang himself to death.

The cameldriver came with his laden camels and his black slaves. His little boy found the dead bird and he buried the little songster in the great Homer's grave. And the rose trembled in the wind. Evening came, the rose folded its petals closer and dreamed. . . .

It was a beautiful day of sunshine. A group of foreigners, Franks,[1] came on pilgrimage to Homer's grave. Among them was a Poet from the North, from the land of mists and northern lights. He picked the rose, pressed it tight in a book and carried it with him to another part of the world, to his distant homeland. And the rose withered from

---

[1] In the Levant, Frank was the usual description of a person of Western nationality—from the Franks who conquered France in the 6th century.

sorrow as it lay in the dark of the book—which he used to open at home, saying, "Here is a rose from Homer's grave." The flower had this dream: a dewdrop fell from its petals on to the poet's grave. The sun came up and the rose bloomed, more beautiful than ever; the day was hot in the heat of Asia. There was a sound of footsteps, some strangers arrived, Franks, as the rose had seen them in its dream, and among them there was a Poet from the North. He picked the rose, pressed a kiss on its fresh mouth and carried it away with him to the land of mists and northern lights.

And then it woke up and shivered in the wind.

Like a mummy the withered rose now rests in his *Iliad* and, as in its dream, it hears him open the book and say, "Here is a rose from Homer's grave."[2]

---

[2] This story was included in the 1862 edition of *Collected Stories*. According to legend, Homer was born and lived in this area. In a note to his poem *The Giaour* Byron said, "The attachment of the nightingale to the rose is a well-known Persian fable. If I mistake not, the 'Bulbul of a thousand tales' is one of his appellations."

The Dardanelles and the Sea of Marmora

We sailed out of the Bay of Smyrna and at dawn the next day we sailed into the Dardanelles, the Hellespont of the ancient world. We steered towards the Asian coast, towards the great city of the Dardanelles on whose fortress there were row upon row of cannon—but they did not greet us. Soldiers in European uniforms, but wearing the red high-crowned fez, peered out between the gun emplacements.

Boats with Turks and their women cruised around our steamship. All the ships around flew the crescent flag, and even a steamer that passed us was Turkish. Its deck was crowded with Muslims and their veiled women. The wind and current was in their favor, the mainsail was raised, smoke whirled from the funnel, thick and black and the ship with its colorful passengers made a speedy passage between the green coasts. Some of our company left us here, but new guests took their place: over one hundred, all Turks with fez or turban and armed with pistols and rifles. An officer, perhaps in his twenties, had his whole harem with him, the wives and servants filled an entire boat when they arrived. I stationed myself near the ladder by which they came on board; three wives, three black female slaves, two children, and a bearer made up the family. The women immediately drew their veils over their faces and even the black slave-women covered their pitch-black beauty. Their bearer, dressed like their lord and master in a military coat, fez on head and slippers over boots, spread out colored cushions by the gunwale, and on these the ladies sat with their backs to us and faces toward the rigging. All of them had gold Moroccan leather boots with red slippers over their feet; they wore baggy silk trousers, a short embroidered shirt and a cone-shaped cap with black trimmings. A large white muslin veil covered breast, neck, chin and mouth, and then hung over the head to the eye-brows, so that nose, and eyes were free. Long dark eye-lashes set off the glint of dark eyes, the whites of which were blue-tinged. the muslin was drawn very tight but was so transparent that one could easily get an idea of the shape of the face. I learned later in Constantinople that it is only when they are old and ugly that the veil is of thicker stuff. One can see the shape and color, the red lips and the shining white teeth when they laugh. The youngest of the women in this group was very beautiful.

Before we sailed all the Turks we got on board had to discharge their pistols and rifles. It was a cheerful noise and echoed from Abydos to Sestos.[1] All of the weapons were laid in a heap in the middle of the ship. In a very few minutes the whole deck—from bowsprit to funnel—was covered with gaily colored cushions and carpets. On these our many Asiatic guests reclined: some smoked tobacco, some drank coffee and yet others opened the shafts of their daggers in which were kept an inkwell and pen. They proceeded to write long pages of Turkish script—but whether these were in prose or verse I cannot say.

Close up to the machine-room chimney lay four sacks of coal and on one of these sat a cheerful young Turk, dressed in blue leather-trimmed fur and wearing a beautiful shawl-turban. He was improvising verse and telling stories to a whole flock of people who squatted on the deck around him, laughing and clapping. There was a merry atmosphere here, quite different from what I had expected from the grave Turks. The Captain and a couple of Franks stood up on the paddle-box and inspected the coastline. A cemetery with white monuments lay on the European side, looking like a field draped with bleaching linen. On the Asiatic side it was lovely spring.

I sat myself among the Turks who were listening to the Improviser and it was obvious how very much more comfortable their clothes were than mine to recline in! Their trousers finished close around the ankles but were baggy around the knees and their jackets sat just as easily. I offered some fruit to the young Turk who was telling the story and he thanked me with a friendly look; his eye-lashes were dark

---

[1] In Asia lay Abydos, in Europe, Sestos, between which Leander swam over the rough stream which separated him from Hero. In the storm the burning lamp held by Love was extinguished, in the storm a burning heart became icy cold. As a gesture, Byron did this same swim. HCA

and long but his eyes were very light blue; they had a very pleasant, but at the same time a somewhat cunning expression. He seized his pen, tore a sheet of paper from his notebook and wrote—while he nodded and smiled at me. Then he handed me the paper with a verse in Turkish written on it. I showed it to a European passenger who knew Turkish and he translated it for me. There stood the young Turk's name—he was going to Wallachia to buy pedigree horses, but first he must see Stamboul! He was making the journey on the excellent steamship *Rhamses* and on this he had met me—who had come from far away, as far as three times to Mecca! I thanked him for the verse and he asked me to write a few words in my language. I wrote a little Danish verse for him, and it was passed around and turned up and down just as I had done with his Turkish poem.

Later I stationed myself by the ship's gunwale, where the Turkish women were sitting; I wanted to look at the coast but I was also looking at the ladies and children. They were eating and had therefore taken their veils from their mouths. They were also looking at me! The youngest and prettiest seemed to be of a very cheerful disposition. She certainly noticed me and whispered something to one of the older people, who preserved the greatest gravity and only replied with a nod. During this mutual observation a young Turk came up and got into conversation with me in French, in the course of which he said, in a half-jesting tone, that it was against the custom of the country to see women without the veil; did I not also think that the husband was regarding me with a very serious look! The older daughter was serving him with pipe and coffee; the younger was running about between him and the ladies. If one wants to be on good terms with the parents one should always make up to the children—that is proverbial wisdom! I would like to have caught the smaller of the two children, to give her some fruit and to joke with her, but she was like a wild kid—she went straight to one of the black girls, clung to her and hid herself in the long veil. The merry little child then laughed, pursed her mouth into a kiss, chortled and then rushed off to her father. The elder sister, perhaps six years old and very pretty, was more tame—a delightful little unveiled Turk, with red leather slippers over gold boots, light blue silk pantaloons wide and baggy around her hips, a red-flowered short tunic with a black velvet jacket on top, which went down to her hips. Her hair hung over her shoulders in two long plaits, entwined with gold coins and on her head was a little cap of gold material. She encouraged her little sister to take the fruit I offered, but she would not. I got the waiter to bring some preserves and straightway the older girl and I became the best of friends. She showed me her toy, a clay drinking pot shaped like a horse, with a little bird behind each ear. If I had been able to speak Turkish I would at once have made up a story about it and have told it to her. I sat her on my lap and she put her small hands on my cheeks and looked at me with such trust and affection that I had to talk to her—I spoke Danish and she laughed and laughed. Never had she heard such an odd language—and she obviously thought it was some sort of Turkish crows-talk that I had invented for her sake! Her fine small nails were painted almost black like the other women's and a black line went down the palm of her hand. I pointed at it and she took one of her long plaits and laid it across my hand in order to make a similiar stripe there. The younger sister waved to her and talked to her but always at a respectful distance. The father called, with the most friendly expression put his hand to his fez in the Frankish fashion and greeted me. He whispered a few words in the little one's ear, she nodded wisely, took a cup of coffee from the waiter's hand and brought it to me. A large Turkish pipe was presented to me, but since I do not smoke tobacco I took the coffee and sat myself down on the cushion beside the friendly husband, whose little daughter's heart I had completely won. The pretty child was called Zuleika and I can truthfully say that as I sailed through the Dardanelles into the Sea of Marmora I received a kiss from a daughter of Asia.

To the left lay the city of Gallipoli. It looked remarkably dark and had almost the character of a northern Swedish town, except of course for the tall white minarets. Each house had a pointed red roof just as in the north, and a little garden; they all looked dark and old-fashioned, with red-painted wooden balconies and bay windows. There was something dark and decaying about the whole place. Several buildings hung over the sea, where the waves were high. The wind was bitterly cold; during the whole of my journey in the south no sea had brought such an icy wind as here—I thought I could feel the marble. There was a lighthouse on both the Asiatic and European sides; low but wild and bare cliffs stretched out by Gallipoli; there were flat green fields as in Denmark and on the coast of Asia were hills, one range after another.

The current and wind were against us. The Sea of Marmora looked dark and foaming. Waves broke against the prow of the ship and showered the Turks who were sitting there. One of them got a proper drenching and he shook his red cloak and took off his three layers of head-gear—of which the outer one was filled with water. As is well known, all Turks have their heads shaved with a long top-knot—by which on the Day of Judgment, the Angel of Life will drag them up out of the grave. This man was wearing first a white night-cap, then a little red fez over it and on top of that a bigger fez with a silk tassel.

For the time being I felt very sea-worthy, but the wind was unbearably cold as in the North. Soon we could see nothing of the coast, neither Europe nor Asia. We were making quickly for the island of Marmora which rose up picturesque and proud in the stormy sea. After dinner we were under its lee where the sea was less strong. The sun was sinking and it lit up the beautiful island with its green trees and shining white hills of marble. I thought of the Thousand and One Nights, and despite the cold, I felt as if I were on the scene of its wonderful stories. I do not think I would have been very surprised if the little clay horse with the bird behind its ear had come to life and grown into a great horse, which could have carried me and little Zuleika and flown with us over to Marmora Island and that, as soon as we touched the ground, she had become a grown maiden, beautiful as she was now as a child and glowing like the sun which had left its rays in her dark eyes. But the clay horse did not come to life and there was no flight. The sea rose higher and higher. I had to go and lie down in my cabin, although it was not more than half-past seven in the evening. The cold sea of Marmora pressed against the ship so that all its ribs creaked and it felt as if the timbers must be wrenched one from the other. Time crept by at a snail's pace. Every time I looked at the clock the hands had scarcely moved a half-hour—it was going to be a long night! And then I went to sleep, while the ship danced over the foam of the *Mare di Marmora!*

Arrival at Constantinople and Pera

April 25, 1841

The whole night had been stormy with squalls: at daybreak the sun was fighting with clouds and mist. Behind us the Sea of Marmora was tumbling with dark green foaming waves—but before us we could see, like a Venice built of Fantasy, great Constantinople, Istanbul of the Turks. Black cypresses and light green leafy trees peeped out in arabesques from between the stone sea of dark-red buildings; in their hundreds tall slender minarets with pointed towers shone against the gray, cloudy sky and the gilded crescents looked like Noah's arks which had come to rest there on the domes of the mosques.

The Bosphorus was invisible. The hilly shores of Asia melted together with the coast of Europe. The sunlight fell like a shower of rays over a part of the great cypress forest. It was the Turks' Asiatic cemetery—about which they say that it is so big that if crops were sown it could supply Constantinople with corn, and its tombstones so many that with them they could build new walls around the city.[1]

We sailed right in under the old walls, which completely merged with the first building we saw: the Fortress, the Seven Towers, in Turkish, *Jedi Kulelev*. Many an earthquake has shaken this building but has never destroyed it.

From the Seven Towers, past the garden of the Seraglio which forms the point of the Golden Horn,[2] a path stretches under the city walls. Small houses and hanging gardens were built on the walls. Turkish boys ran about, shrieking and playing up there.

Under the Seraglio garden the path became smaller, but the wall was high and quite white, with small swaying houses with latticed

---

[1] The headland here by Scutari is the place where legend says Io landed when, turned into a cow, she fled from Juno. HCA.

[2] Constantinople is built in the shape of a cornucopia, from which comes the name, Golden Horn. HCA.

windows shining with gold and silver. The garden and walls lay dreaming—as in a fairy tale. The old Seraglio[3] is a dark red, quite handsome building, but there is something heavy about it in comparison with its surroundings. The new Seraglio looks friendly and inviting, with beautiful pavilions, whose precious marble columns support the decorative projecting roofs.

We turned round the Golden Horn, past Leander's tower[4] and now were in the harbor which stretches deep in to the "sweet waters."[5] On the left side, Constantinople greeted us, to the right Galata and the higher-lying Pera, whose round tower reached up high into the sky among the driving clouds. Big ships made a whole forest of masts in the broad bay. A mass of boats, most of them thin and small—like native canoes—with rowers and passengers lying in the bottom, flew past, arrow-swift. There was such a yelling, shouting, whistling and humming that, compared with this, the noise in the Bay of Naples almost seemed to be like a wake! Old yellow-brown Turks with great colored turbans and bare arms, all shouting together, swung their oars and invited us to step into their boat. My luggage was thrown down and I went after it and now we went with firm strokes of the oars towards the shore, which was decorated with boats and small craft; the way on to the land was over their decks. I offered the oarsman a silver coin, the value of which I was not really as yet clear about. He shook his head, took from his pocket quite a small coin, showed it to me and assured me that he could not take any higher payment. So honest are the Turks! And every day during my stay here I had more and more proof of this. The Turks are the most good-hearted and honorable people.

---

[3] On the square where Byzas raised temples for Neptune and Aphrodite, Constantine built churches to the Mother of God and the Holy Barbara. Where these temples and churches stood is now the Seraglio. One of the springs that was holy to the Christians still runs from the garden out through the wall.
[4] The Turks call it the Maiden's Tower and connect it with the story of a Greek princess who was held prisoner here by her father, but freed by the Arab hero Heschan. In our day it was used as a lighthouse. This is what the Franks called the beautiful valley which forms the northern boundary of the harbor and is a pleasure garden for the people of Constantinople and its suburbs. HCA.
[5] This is what the Franks called the beautiful valley which forms the northern boundary of the harbor and is a pleasure garden for the people of Constantinople and its suburbs. HCA.

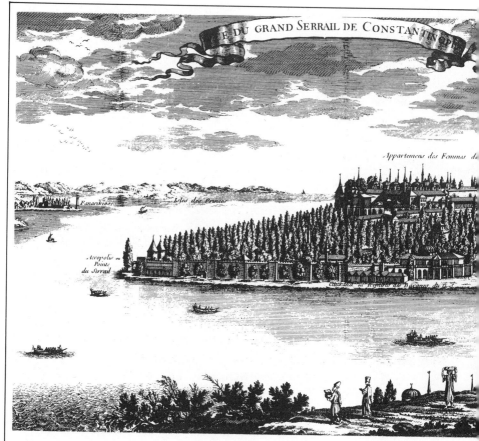

View of the Grand Seraglio of Constantinople. Hagia Sophia, the great landmark of Constantinople, is at far right; the gardens of the Seraglio form the point of the

A ruddy-brown, muscle-strong Turk offered to carry my baggage. Quickly he slung a cord around my trunk, over-night bag and hat-box, threw the load on to his shoulders and ambled off, nodding his head continuously when I told him the name of the hotel where I intended to stay.

We came into a crooked street, where every house was a shop with vegetables, bread, meat or clothes. We met all nationalities. The way

Golden Horn on the left. The apartments of the women of the harem are at the top of the hill. MUSEUM OF TURKISH AND ISLAMIC ART

went through the narrow gate of Galata into Pera. No one asked about passports.[6] The road ran steeply up and was just as narrow and just as badly paved as that in Galata. We passed some guards—young, dark brown lads in narrow blue trousers and jackets, white bandoleers and

---

[6] It was the same with my arrival in Greece. On the other hand, on departure my baggage and that of every passenger was examined in Piraeus—to see that we were not smuggling out statues or columns.

red fez; they lay almost on their stomachs on the road and read their prayers. An hour-glass stood beside them.

We passed Turkish cafés; fountains splashed in the open rooms. The monastery of the Whirling Dervishes, with gilded inscriptions from the Koran engraved in the wall over the gate, lay on our way through the very narrow main street. The houses had two or three stories, all with bay windows. The side streets are even more narrow; the buildings seem to meet overhead—when it rains one would scarcely need an umbrella.

What a crowd! And in the middle of the throng there danced a Bulgarian peasant, a red skull-cap on his head, wretched sandals on his feet and, for the rest, a sheepskin coat. He danced like a bear, which jumps on its back legs. Another Bulgarian blew bagpipes as an accompaniment. Porters dragged great blocks of marble which hung on staves—six to eight brown, muscular fellows were on the job, continuously yelling their "Make Way!" Armenian priests with mourning bands flying from their hats came towards us; we could hear a mumbled song; a young Greek girl was being buried; she lay in her ordinary clothes and with uncovered face in an open coffin, decorated with flowers. Three Greek priests and two small boys with lighted candles walked in front.

Decorated wagons which looked like paper boxes, painted gold back and front, and with long waving curtains through which veiled women peered out, bumped over the uneven cobbles. Horses and donkeys, laden with timbers and beams which trailed behind them down to the road, forced their way through the throng.

At last we got to the *Hotel de la France*, to Herr Blondel; as soon as one was in the door there was a feeling of European order and comfort. French and Italian waiters sprang up and down the stairs, pleasant rooms opened up, one from the other, and at the *table d'hôte* one ate as in any other good hotel in the capitals of Europe. The company was very colorful.[7] Most of the Franks, who had come from

---

[7] Here Andersen met Achille Laurent in this hotel. "Here in the hotel lives a very fat Frenchman who always wore Turkish clothes," Andersen wrote. Laurent was the author of *Relation historique de Syrie depuis 1840 jusqau 1842.*

trips in Asia Minor, were still wearing Asiatic costume, in which they had felt safer. A couple of Prussian officers serving in the Sultan's army were in Turkish military cloaks with the high crowned fez. The noise from the street came in to us. We could hear the whine of the Bulgarian's bagpipes, but this was out-screeched by the nasal song of some poor unveiled women out from the hills; and then there came the roar of the loud Janissary[8] music of the Turkish soldiers, coming home from maneuvers. I knew that tune—it was the gallop from Auber's opera, *Gustav III*.

---

[8] Janissary music was Turkish military music played by a band consisting of shrill fifes, oboes, cymbals, triangles and drums.

The Bazaars

April 25–May 4, 1841, Constantinople

First of all in Constantinople the foreigner should visit the bazaars—for there, in an instant, he is in the heart of this incredible city. One is overwhelmed by the sights, the splendor and the tumult. It is a bee-hive one enters, but every bee is a Persian, an Armenian, an Egyptian, a Greek. Orient and Occident hold a great market here. Such a throng, such variety of costume, and such a diversity of goods for sale is seen nowhere else.

When one sails from Pera over the bay and lands in Constantinople, the street leading to the bazaars goes straight up, narrow, crooked and winding. The ground floors of the houses on each side are like the wooden stalls in our markets. One can look straight into the workshop of the shoemaker and cabinet-maker. One feels as if he were walking right through the kitchen and the bakery—such is the cooking, baking, steaming and the smell from the ovens and chimneys in the open houses. Bread and many other kinds of food are on display.

We are now standing outside the Grand Bazaar, around which branch out small, half-covered streets: one quarter offers all sorts of vegetables and fruit, both fresh and preserved; another quarter has shell fish and other fish of the most vaired colors and shapes. Great pieces of canvas or old carpet are drawn over the street from stall to stall like a roof. The paving is bad and a drain runs through the middle of the street.

A long entrance hall, mostly of wood and quite filled with pipe-heads, pipe stems and mouth pieces of amber leads into the bazaar, which is made of thick, fire-proof walls. It is a whole roofed-in city. Every group has its own quarter here—Jews, Egyptians and so on. Each kind of business has its own street, every craft its own—the shoemakers, saddlemakers and others, to infinity! Every street has an arch painted with flowers and texts from the Koran. The light comes down from above. Stall is stuck to stall, looking like an upturned packing case. In the back—in the thick wall—an opening is cut where the goods not on display are stored.

The Egyptian quarter looks like a complete pharmacy, stretching through two streets. All the spices of India and Arabia, the herbs and roots for medicine and precious dyes send out a mixed perfume. A yellowish-brown Egyptian in a long robe stands behind the counter; he looks the very picture of an alchemist.

Another vaulted arch looks as if it must be the entrance to the world's armory. And then there is the archway of the saddlemakers; saddles and drums of Moroccan leather and buffalo-skin, from the most intricately and artistically sewn to the most simple, almost clumsy, hang on the walls and lie spread out on counter and floor.

Another archway is the jewelers'—good necklaces glitter, bracelets shine, precious rings and expensive jewels dazzle the eye.

Now one comes to the perfumes—pure and concentrated; there is a smell of attar of roses. Here they sell musk-purses, frankincense and scented rats' tails. We go into the next archway and see nothing but boots and shoes, all colors, all shapes, slippers shining with pearls and real embroidery. Another archway crosses close by here and in this are concentrated haberdashery, muslins, handkerchiefs embroidered with big gold flowers, beautiful materials. In the next arch there is the flash of weapons: damascene blades, daggers, knives, rifles and pistols.

It is very interesting to note the characteristic which each nationality reveals of itself here. The Turk sits, serious and grave, with his long pipe in his mouth; the Jew and the Greek are busy—they shout and wave. Meanwhile the motley human throng masses its way through the criss-cross arches, the Persians with their heavy, pointed caps, the Armenians with their upside-down cone-shaped black hats, the Bulgarians in sheepskin coats, Jews with a tattered shawl around a black high-crowned turban, smart Greeks and veiled women—what a busyness there is. And through it there rides, very gravely, a distinguished Turk, who looks neither to right nor left.

At a given signal in the evening both sellers and buyers go away.

A kind of watchman, whose job it is to keep guard in the bazaars, closes all the entrances and opens them again at a fixed time the next morning. The salesmen find their stalls exactly as they left them. During the days an individual booth is closed simply by the owner hanging a net in front or by drawing a couple of strands of twine across. No one dares to steal.

Compared with the bazaars of Constantinople, the beautiful shops of the Palais Royale (in Paris) are only like a heavily painted *grisette*— as compared with a daughter of the Orient in her rich costume, her hair fragrant with attar of roses and myrrh.

A Ramble Through Constantinople

We have seen the bazaars, the heart of old Istanbul; we will take a little walk and begin with what used to be called "the forbidden way" for the Christians. We will go first to the slave-market[1] and then go on to one of the mosques. Permission is fairly easy to get but the presents that have to be offered to the various officials, through whose hands this authority goes, mount up to no small sum of money. But among the foreigners in Pera there is often an Ambassador or wealthy man who will gladly pay this tribute. Hired servants always know when such an opportunity occurs and then you attach yourself to the person who has the license, which is always made out for the Personage and his retinue.

In this way we are attached to the company of a wealthy American; but we must be on horse-back because this looks more imposing and the Turks respect pomp and splendor. A couple of soldiers, also mounted, lead the procession.

Not far from the Grand Bazaar there is a square, surrounded by wooden buildings which form an open gallery. The projecting roof is supported by timbers. Inside the long gallery are small rooms where the merchants have their wares—and these wares are human beings, black and white female slaves.

Now we are in this square; the sun is shining, straw mats are spread out under the green trees and there sit and lie the daughters of Asia. A young mother is suckling her child—the two will not be parted. On the stairway up to the gallery sits a fourteen-year old Negro girl; she is as good as naked. An old Turk is looking her over; he has taken her leg in his hand—she laughs and shows her shining white teeth.

A young Turk with a fiery look comes along. Four slaves follow him, two old Jewish women bargain with him. Some lovely-looking

---

[1] In addition to this market there is another in Topschana for the slave-women and one for the male slaves out by the Seven Towers. HCA.

girls have arrived—he wants to see them dance, hear them sing and then make his choice and buy!

We stop at the church of Santa Sophia. It is a heavy irregular building. Constantine the Great built it and dedicated it to Holy Wisdom—*Hagia Sophia*; unique relics were preserved here: the well

Turkish Tombs drawn by Hans Christian Andersen during his visit to Constantinople in 1841. PHOTO COLLECTION GRACE THORNTON.

Street Scene in Constantinople. Andersen remarked on narrow streets in which the houses "seem to meet overhead" and "fantastic buildings where everything is marble and gold." NEW YORK PUBLIC LIBRARY PICTURE COLLECTION.

from Samaria, three doors made of timbers from Noah's ark, petrified trumpets said to have been used at the siege of Jericho, but all these have disappeared. *Hagia Sophia* was twice destroyed by fire and once in an earthquake, but always it rose up again, splendid as ever. During the night of Ramadan when the great dome is blazing with the light and the whole congregation in their best clothes lie stretched out, their faces to the ground, the church dreams about the Imperial coronations, nuptials, synods and church assemblies, dreams of that night of terror when its doors were forced open and the Christian altars were desecrated. "There is no God but God and Mohammed is his Prophet"— it hears this still, as it heard it from the lips of the Emperor Mehemet[2] that night when it was turned into a mosque. What wonderful dreams— which concern the whole history of mankind!

Do you also have a dream of the future, *Hagia Sophia*—do you have a presentiment, perhaps shared by the people herein, that the defaced Christian cross on the door will one day be renewed? Will the altar be moved from the corner facing Mecca and once more find its place to the East? The Moslem points to a walled-up door in the topmost gallery of the church and whispers a legend from that night—how a Christian priest was cut down before the altar behind that door and, sometime, when the Christians are again the Rulers here and the seed of Ishmael retreats to Asia, then every stone in this door will fall and the Christian priest will stand there again and sing the rest of the Mass, from the point at which he was stopped when the death-blow fell. When the Mass ends then the dead man will vanish and through the Church will ring out the Christian hymns. . . .

It is odd to walk in here, followed by armed men and looked at with angry eyes by the praying congregation—as if we were damned souls. . . .

There are magnificent columns here. Eight of them, of porphyry, once stood under the dome of the Temple of the Sun at Baalbek; the green ones were brought here from the Temple of Diana at Ephesus. Under the dome one reads, in letters five yards high, a text from the Koran—"God is the Light of Heaven and Earth."

Do not look so angrily at us, old Priest—your God is also our God; the Temple of Nature is the House of God for all of us: you kneel towards Mecca, we face East; God is the Light of Heaven and the World, He illuminates every soul and heart!

---

[2] The Emperor Mehemet (Mohammed) II: (1430–1481): responsible for the Fall of Constantinople in 1453 and the transformation of Santa Sophia into a mosque.

We leave *Hagia Sophia* and a short street leads us to Almeidan, the biggest and most beautiful square in Constantinople. But once upon a time it was far more beautiful. For here was the Hippodrome, which Constantine embellished with colonnades and statues; here were the proud bronze horses which are now in Venice over the entrance to the Church of St. Mark's.[3] Here was the colossal statue of Hercules— of which every finger was the size of a human being. Only three memorials of ancient days are found here now—the nearest is a little column made up of three entwined copper snakes; once it was the base of the Oracle's tripod in Delphi.[4] The Turks regarded it as a talisman for the Greek kingdom and for this reason Mehemet II cut off one of the snake's heads with his battle-axe. The English stole the other two.

A few steps away is an obelisk of porphyry, covered with hieroglyphics. It came from Egypt via Athens and stands here, unchanged, as if protected by invisible Egyptian gods.

The third relic here is a four-sided column of mighty stone that threatens to fall—it is Constantine's column. Once it was decorated with copper plates, gilded over, but now only the iron rings that held the plates together are to be seen.

These are the remains of the splendor of the Hippodrome—but still this is the most beautiful square in the city. Its expanse and Sultan Achmed's mosque charm our eyes. Behind the shining white walls with gilded lattice windows, tall plane trees and cypresses rise up; inside fountains splash, with gilded memorial pillars. It is a small grove where motley clad Moslems and women still stroll. Broad steps lead up to Achmed's mosque, where everything is marble, even the six high minarets. Golden balls gleam on the cupolas, the crescent shines on the Minarets. It is a wonderful sight.

And now we must leave it; a crooked little street leads us to a

---

[3] The horses came from Athens to Chios and then to Constantinople from where they were taken to Venice. Napoleon had them taken to Paris and now they are back in Venice. HCA.
[4] The base of the Oracle's tripod: the snake column from Delphi was not from the Oracle's tripod but from the tripod commemorating the defeat of the Persians at Platea in 479 BC; it was made from the spoils of the battle and was mentioned by various ancient authors, including Herodotus. The surviving snake's head is in the Archaeological Museum in Istanbul.

fantastic building where everything is marble and gold. Plane trees, cypresses and rose hedges in flower make a little garden behind the walls, which are decorated with beautiful windows and artistic carved work. The building itself is surely Fata Morgana's own bedroom—it is very light and airy although built of marble; the pillars and ceiling and cornices glow with ornamentation and color. We mount the stairs which go around the whole building, look in through one of the big window panes between the gilded lattice and see in to a round, airy room. The eye is dazzled by oriental splendor! Is it a bridal chamber for the first Pascha of the land? No, it is a tomb! It is the grave of Sultan Mahmud. In the center of the floor stands his coffin, covered with precious multi-colored shawls. His rich turban, sparkling with jewels and with a feather that seems to be made out of the rays of the sun, lies on the coffin; round about are grouped smaller coffins in each of which lie the remains of one of his children, one of his concubines. All are covered with rich tapestries; two priests stare out at us and raise threatening hands.

"Christians may not look upon the grave of a Believer!" they say. The incense bowl is swung, the bluish smoke rises in the rays of the sun, towards the magnificent ceiling.

Over the coffin of Mahmud, when it was brought here, a tent was raised. Rich and poor were granted access—old men wept, so beloved was he, the man who overthrew the Janissaries, introduced Frankish discipline and dress.

The Dancing Dervishes

It is well-known that the Turks, that is to say the rude mass of the nation, regard all the mentally deranged as inspired by a divine spirit. Therefore the mad have a place in the mosques; the dreadful *Isawi*[1] are the objects of respect and awe and so are the Dervishes with their dance, which is veritable self-torture.

The Dervishes who have their monastery in Scutari are called *Ruhanis* which means "the howling ones." The Dervishes in Pera are called *Mevlevis*, which means "whirling"—they usually dance on Thursdays and Fridays. I went to see some of these dances and will try to give a description of them and of the impression the whole ceremony in their cloisters made upon me.

We went over the Bosphorus to Scutari, a city of some 150,000 people—about half as many as Copenhagen—but regarded only as a suburb of Constantinople. Here everything is old Mohammedan. The orthodox Turks—if one may dare to call them that—live here. A couple of heavily armed, half naked Arabs drove their laden camels from the shore through the main street, out towards the great cemetery. We followed them and stopped on the outskirts of the town, by a poor, insignificant house—so far as I remember it was half-timbered; this was the Dervishes' monastery.

The door was not yet open; we had come too early, so we went to one of the nearby Turkish cafés which border the mile-long cypress wood where the dead rest. Outside the cafés sat a crowd of Turks, military and civil; some were here to take part in the dance of the Dervishes or, like us, just to watch. A hideous old dwarf was sitting there—he was an ardent *Ruhani* I was told and I should soon see him among the dancers. He was reputed to be very rich and to have twelve beautiful wives in his harem. He had his little son with

[1] Isawa is an order of Dervishes, a Moslem religious brotherhood that was founded about 1500 A.D.

him in the café—an attractive child, the same height as his father.

At last the monastery door was opened. We went in and entered a broad anteroom, which was divided into two by a hanging carpet. Everyone had to take off his shoes or boots which were put behind the curtain.

My companion took a pair of moroccan leather slippers out of his pocket, put them on over his boots and went in like that, but the Turks looked angrily at him and muttered to each other. I had straps sewn fast in my trouser legs so it was difficult to take my boots off, but since one should always follow the customs of the country or keep out, I quickly took a knife, cut the straps and walked, like the Turks, in my stockinged feet. An old man with a turban clapped me on the shoulder, nodded gently and said something which my interpreter translated for me: I was a good man who respected religion and deserved to be a Turk! "God give you Light" was his last word.

I now entered the temple itself—if it can be called that. It was a square room; up above there was a heavily latticed gallery for the female spectators and down below a barrier of unplaned planks was set around the dancing place. For the moment this was covered with red, white and blue colored skins, on which a crowd of Dervishes lay on their stomachs. They were dressed in the ordinary costume of the Turks, although there were many here in the newly prescribed costume: military great-coat and the high large fez. They touched the floor with their foreheads; but now and then they raised their heads—and then, as if something had frightened them, they quickly bent them down again. I stood in my stockings on the cold stone floor and fidgeted about, trying to put one foot on the instep of the other to maintain some warmth; it was not at all comfortable.

On the center wall there hung great framed turkish texts and pictures of buildings, as well as tambourines, cymbals and iron scourges with sharp spikes—to take the skin off with! In the middle of the wall, as in Turkish mosques, there was a niche which served as an altar, in front of which stood a priest with a long white beard, in blue clothing and green turban. He swung a censer, and in an incredibly guttural tone chanted some Turkish words. Now solo voices began a song with

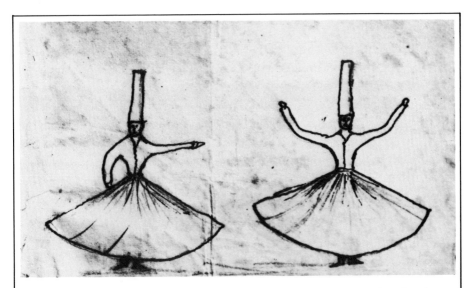

The Dancing Dervishes. Drawing by Hans Christian Andersen. This sketch appeared in a letter written to a friend at home describing the visit to Scutari. PHOTO COLLECTION GRACE THORNTON.

a choir—I say a song but that is not the right word for it. It was a sound that had something peculiarly wild about it, with different varying rhythms—a sort of scale, an incredible run in the throat, rather as if a savage with a musical ear, after hearing for the first time a great bravura-aria, wanted in his own fashion to reproduce the artificial song. It was more painful to hear than really unmelodious.

After the Dervishes had touched the floor several times with their foreheads, they rose, kissed the priest's hands and stationed themselves in a half circle along the barrier, behind which the spectators were standing.

The dance began and at that moment there entered a man, who was the most horrible I had yet seen. Two Dervishes from Pera, recognizable by their high-crowned, brimless felt hats, escorted him. My interpreter said he was a hermit from the district around Medina. I have never seen a human being from whose eyes madness shone so clearly as it did here. The other dancers had laid their turbans and fez in front of the niche and each one had put on a white felt skull-cap. The hermit was wearing such a cap; long coarse black hair hung down over his shoulders and back; he had a white cape on which two winged horses were sewn with red thread. He positioned himself in the middle of the half circle. They all stood as if their feet were nailed fast, but they set their other limbs in motion—as in a steam engine. Every joint moved in the same direction and in time, first forward then back, now right, now left and all of it under a song or to patter—whatever it could be called—first slowly and then in faster and faster tempo—the song as well as the movement. The dancers got into wild, almost obscene postures.

Two young Turks sat on their haunches outside the half-circle and led the song, which rose continuously on one note on the third syllable—they went through the whole family of Mohammed from Abdallah to Mohammed and the choir answered *"La illah! ilallah!"* It sounded in the end like a muffled shriek, a snort or death-rattle. Some were deathly pale, others looked as if blood and water were pouring from their faces. The hermit cast off his great cape and now stood in a red woolen blouse with long sleeves covering his hands, and with bare legs. Soon he was seized with madness and tore the tight blouse into pieces; he slashed at his chest with his bare arms—one hand was withered; probably he had, once upon a time, deformed it himself. His mouth was a bloody gash, his lips were both cut and the white teeth seemed to grin—it was a dreadful sight! Blood started up from his mouth, his eyes rolled, the veins in his forehead swelled up. The dance got wilder and wilder and yet no one moved an inch from his place. The dancers seemed not to be human beings but machines; they no longer uttered words—these were lost in shrieks—"Jehova" sounded like *"Je-hu."* In the other sentences *"Ja-med"*—oh help!—sounded clearly. It was like a death stroke, it was dreadful and the longer I looked at the dancers, the more I felt as if I were in a madhouse among raving lunatics. *"Ja-hu, ja-hu"* they screamed, shrieking, wild.

My companion whispered to me, "For heaven's sake, don't laugh—or we will be in trouble. They'll murder us!" "Laugh?" I replied, "I can't even weep! It is harrowing, it is horrible—I can't bear it any longer," and quickly I made for the exit and at that moment a couple of the dancers sank to the ground.

Outside in the street I could still hear the wild shout, *"Ja-hu, ja-hu!"*

How lovely, how warm it was out there in the clear sunshine. The light boat, splinter-thin, goes from the coast of Asia towards Europe, over the strong currents, past sailing ships and boats—the slightest bump and we could easily turn over, but I did not think about that; we had come from the house of terror—and everything out here was natural and life-loving. The dance of the Dervishes in Scutari hung in my memory like the picture of a madhouse.

The Birthday of Mohammed

The fourth of May is the Prophet's birthday; the festivities begin the evening before, which is without doubt the most beautiful part of the celebrations. There was moonlight, but even in these circumstances the Ottoman police-law commands everyone who goes out after sunset to carry a light in a lantern if he does not wish to be arrested. I had to go along with this; neither moonshine nor the police-law could be changed.

A young Russian, Aderhas, and I decided to go together without a guide, but furnished with a light in a large paper lantern, we set out to see the illuminations in honor of the Prophet. We walked through one of Pera's narrow side-streets, and there before us was a sight so splendid, so fantastic and beautiful—such as in the North one can only see in a wonderful dream. From the row of houses where we stood and deep down towards the bay, there stretched a vast cemetery—that is to say a cypress wood with great close-set trees. Coal-black night rested therein. Under the tall trees, over uneven slopes, the foot-path twists, downward—as the feet of men and the hooves of horses have beaten it out. Here and there a red or blue light moved, then disappeared and as quickly re-appeared in the black ground. A few lonely houses lie there in the cemetery; lights shone out from the upper storeys or were set out on the open balconies.

The bay, filled with ships and blue as a Damascene blade, shone over the tops of the cypresses. Two of the biggest ships were dressed over-all with burning lamps, which shone around the cannon emplacements by the gunwale and mast; they hung in the rigging and turned it into a shining net. In front lay great Constantinople itself with its countless minarets, all circled round with garlands of lamps; the sky was still red from the setting sun, but clear and transparent.

Near to where we stood there was not a single person to be seen. It was lonely and still. We walked down between the cypresses; a nightingale sang its piercing song and turtle doves cooed in the darkness of the trees. We passed a little guard-house, made of wood and painted red; a small fire had been lit in front between the grave-stones and soldiers lay around it. They were dressed in European fashion, but their features and complexion said that they were of the lineage of Ishmael, children of the desert. With long pipes in their mouths, they lay and listened to what was being told; it was about the birth of Mohammed. The nightingale translated it for us, otherwise we would not have understood.

"La Illah, ilallah"—"There is no God but God!" In the city of Mecca merchants came together for the sake of trade. There came Indians and Persians, there came Egyptians and Syrians. In the temple *Kaaba* each had his Picture of God and a son of the race of Ishmael performed one of the most useful tasks there—that of providing pilgrims with food and drink. In his piety he wanted, like Abraham, to sacrifice his son, but the soothsayer bade the handsome Abdallah live and to offer a hundred camels for him. *La Illah Ilallah!* And Abdallah grew and became so beautiful that hundreds of girls died for love of him. The flame of the Prophet shone from his brow, the flame which from the day of Creation went hidden from generation to generation until the Prophet was born, Mohammed, the Last and the First. The soothsayer Fatima saw this flame and she offered hundreds of camels for his embrace, but he took Emina to his bosom and that same night the Prophet's flame vanished from his brow and burned under Emina's heart. *La Illah Ilallah!* Nine months passed and never have the flowers of the earth smelled so sweet as then, never has the fruit on the branch swelled up so full of juice. Then the rocks shook, the Sava sea sank into the earth, the pictures of the gods were destroyed in the temple and the demons who would storm Heaven fell like millions of shooting stars. For Mohammed the Prophet was born that night. *La Illah, ilallah!*

The nightingale translated this story for us and the nightingale understands Turkish just as well as he understands Danish.

We went under the tower of Pera out to the monastery of the Whirling Dervishes and a vast panorama opened up. The whole of the Sea of Marmora and the mountains of Asis lay shining in the moonlight and in the middle-ground Scutari rose up, its minarets gleaming with lamps like those of Constantinople. And here in particular the Sophia Mosque stood out with its four minarets, and the Mosque of Achmed with its six—each with two or three twinkling garlands of stars. They seemed to encircle the gardens of the seraglio which stretched out, dark as a starless night, down towards the Bosphorus. Not a light showed in the Sultana's buildings along the shore, but at the point of the Golden Horn there was planted a flaming sword, which threw its red glare out over the water. Innumerable small boats, each with its red, blue or green paper lanterns traveled like fireflies between the two continents. All the great warships gleamed with lights; one could see the rigging and masts on every ship. Everything looked as if it were outlined with flame. Scutari and Istanbul seemed to be linked together by the gleaming water and the colored points of flame—it was the home of story, the city of fantasy. Everything was enveloped in a magic light—only on two points night lay with all its hidden secrecy: in Asia it was on the great cemetery behind Scutari, and in Europe it was in the garden of the seraglio. Both places lay dreaming in dark night.

In the streets of Pera there was a throng of Greeks, Jews and Franks, each with his lantern or candle; like an Oriental "Moccoli"[1]; but they were in costumes far more correct, richer and more colorful than in Rome's Corso on the last night of Carnival. In front of the palaces of the foreign Ministers lamps burned, set up in pyramids or representing the name of Mohammed in a great "M." At nine-o'clock cannon were fired from all the ships; everything shook as under the most violent sea-battle, every window rattled, shot followed shot, celebrating the hour of the Prophet's birth.

I went to sleep during the shooting and woke up early to the same uproar. Cheerful music from Rossini and Donizetti echoed through the streets as troops marched off to parade between the Seraglio and the Achmed Mosque, from where the Sultan's great procession was to start.

---

[1] Moccoli were the tiny lighted candles carried in the streets of Rome during the Carnival.

Our Danish Consul, Romani—an Italian—came to fetch me. A young Turk with pistols in his belt and carrying two long tobacco pipes, went ahead of us; an old Armenian in a loose swinging dark blue caftan, black vase-shaped hat on his shaven head, carried our cloaks after us, and in this way we proceeded through the main street of Pera down to Galata. The attendants went in one boat and we two in another—and now we went over the Bay, arrow-swift between the hundreds of other boats, whose rowers continuously screamed and shouted so that one should not collide with and sink the other's light vessel. At the landing place in Constantinople a mass of gondolas formed a great rocking bridge over which we had to jump in order to reach fast land, which was banked up with half-rotten planks and timbers. It was very crowded but soon we got into a broader side-street where there were plenty of people—but all the same, place and room enough. Groups of veiled women were taking the same route as we were, and soon we were under the walls of the Seraglio which, on the city side, are very high and look like the walls of an old fortress. Here and there is a tower with a little iron door which looks as if it had never been opened—grass and climbing plants hung over the hinges! Great old trees stretched their leafy branches out over the walls—one could believe that this was the boundary of the enchanted wood with the sleeping princess.

We selected our place outside the Sophia Mosque, between the great fountain and the entrance to the seraglio. From here the Sophia Mosque with its many domes and side-buildings has something that reminds one of a great flower-bulb, which has put out a mass of small bulbs all around it. The terraces in front were crowded with Turkish women and children; their shining white veils gave the whole a festive air.

Between the fountain and the great gate which led into the first court of the Seraglio two long forms had been made of planks laid on barrels and tables, one higher than the other. Both were covered with cushions and carpets and on these veiled Turkish women of the sim-plest class were reclining. Old Turks, Persians and a number of foreigners, whose unveiled women were the subject of great curiosity, sat on the higher part of the scaffolding. Now there came several regiments of Turkish soldiers, all in European uniforms with tight trousers and short jackets, white bandoleer crossed over chest and shoulder and all with the stiff red fez on head. The guard was very well turned out: they had new uniforms, stiff cravats and that day, for the first time so I heard, white gloves. The other regiments, on the other hand, looked really dreadful. I will not talk about the different complexions and colors—white, brown and coal-black—but there were indeed both halt and club-footed soldiers. The European uniform was too tight for them and a lot of them had therefore cut the seams of the sleeves up over the elbow or slashed the trouser legs around the knees, so that they could move more freely—but, as a result, a bare elbow stuck out and during the march a red or coal-black knee appeared out of the blue trousers. One lot gave an especially fine performance: I could really call it the bare-legged Regiment, because some had only one boot and one shoe and others went completely bare-legged and in slippers—and each slipper in a different color too! To clashing music they all marched into the Seraglio and after they had filed past the Sultan, back they came and stationed themselves in rows on each side of the street; Ethiopians and Bulgars stood side by side, the Bedouin was neighbor to the shepherd's son from the Balkan hills.

The procession was due to begin at ten o'clock, but it was nearly twelve before it pleased the Sultan to leave the Seraglio. The sun burned down with summer heat. One cup of coffee after another was drunk, the wooden "scaffolding" twice collapsed and all the Turkish women rolled together in a heap! It was a long time to wait. Some years ago in this place it was the custom to throw out to the dogs the heads of those who had been executed in the Seraglio court; now it all looked very peaceful.

At last there was a sound of cannon from the garden of the Seraglio and the procession began. At the head was a mounted music corps. Even the man with the cymbals and the man with the big drum were on horseback. The reins lay loose round the horse's neck while the cymbals glinted in the sun. Then came the guard which, quite truthfully, looked as good as any guard in Christendom. Then there was a troop of beautiful horses, all without riders, but decked with wonderful saddle-cloths, red, blue and green—sewn all over with precious stones. The horses seemed to dance on their fine strong legs; they stretched their necks, with the long manes; their red nostrils quivered. A troop of mounted young officers followed, all in European style uniform, in great-coat and fez. After them came officials, military and civil, all in the same kind of dress, and then the country's Grand Vizier, a man with a long white beard. At different places in the street bands of musicians were stationed. One played after another—especially numbers from Rossini's *William Tell*. Suddenly these stopped and the favorite march of the young Sultan began. It was composed by the brother of Donizetti who is the master of court music here.

The Sultan arrived. Before him there was a train of Arab horses, with even more beautiful trappings than the ones we had seen before. There were bows of rubies and emeralds by the horses' ears, the moroccan leather reins were sewn with sparkling stones and the saddles and cloths were embroidered with pearls and other jewels. It was the sort of splendor that the genie of the lamp created for Aladdin.

The young, nineteen year old Sultan, Abdul Mesched,[2] sat on a beautiful Arab horse, surrounded by a flock of young men all on foot and all as handsome as if they had been the women of the Orient who had dared to go out unveiled. Each carried a green feather fan in his hand. The Sultan was wearing a green coat, buttoned over the chest and without any kind of adornment—except for a great jewel and a bird of Paradise feather on his red fez. He looked very pale and thin, had a rather unhappy expression, and kept his dark eyes fastened on the sightseers, especially on the Europeans. We took off our hats in greetings. The soldiers shouted loudly, "Long live the Emperor," but he made not the slightest movement in response. "Why does he not greet us?" I asked the young man beside me, "he must have noticed that we took our hats off." "He looked at you," answered the Turk, "he looked at you very closely!" We had to be content with that—

---

[2] Abdul Mesched (1823–1861) succeeded his father in 1839. He initiated a number of reforms, including improved status for Christians in the Ottoman Empire.

View of Constantinople and the Golden Horn. Andersen called the sight from the
hill looking out to the Golden Horn "so splendid, so fantastic and beautiful—such

as in the North one can only see in a wonderful dream."

as if it were as good as the best greeting. I told the Turk that all
Frankish princes gave greetings with heads bared—just as we greeted
them. This seemed to him to be like a fairy story. He thought I was
making it up.

The Pashas and the other great men of the land followed after, with
the Frankish officers in Turkish service and then a crowd of Turkish
men and women bringing up the rear of the procession. There was a
great crowd and it was very noisy. Half-naked street urchins, with
tattered turbans, and old beggar women veiled in rags but with moroccan leather slippers and colored trousers, forced their way screaming
through the crowd. *Allah Akbar*—God is Great! they wailed, and on
both sides, waving like reeds on a river-bank, were the shining bayonets. Everywhere when the Europeans wanted to pass, the officers
of the military guards of honor came forward at once with great courtesy
and made a way for them. They moved aside their brothers in the
Faith—who stared at the honored Franks while repeating the cry *Allah
Akbar!*

A Visit and Departure

At the home of Ali Effendi and the Imperial interpreter, Saphet—both of whom live in the same building, which bears the name of the *Sublime Porte*—I saw for the first time the inside of a Turkish house. On the stairways and in the long corridors, which were covered with straw matting, there was a throng of Europeans, Asiatics and Moslems, as well as poor women, with petitions in their hands. Soldiers went around with short heavy swords. Everyone who came had first to take off his boots or shoes and put on slippers.

In front of the entrances, which were hung with long carpets, armed attendants kept guard. Inside the room divans, the main items of furniture, were placed round the walls. Ali Effendi was pleased to discuss with me Lamartine's journey to the Orient and he asked me if I intended to write about my stay here and the impression the sight of Constantinople had made upon me. I told him that I found the situation the most beautiful in the world, that the view far surpassed that of Naples, but that we in the North had a city that offered something very much like Constantinople. And I described Stockholm which, seen from Mosebakken, has something of the prospect that Constantinople offers from the Pera tower out towards the sweet waters. That part of Stockholm which is called Sødermalmen shows us red-painted wooden houses, cupolas on the churches, fir trees and hanging birches—all very Turkish—only the minarets are missing. During our conversation he asked me how many days' journey Stockholm lay from the capital of my fatherland and what difference there was between the languages of the two places. Saphet was less talkative, but very attentive and seemed to be quite Europeanized. Thick coffee and pipes with good tobacco was presented. I, who never smoke tobacco, had out of politeness to put the pipe into my mouth. It was the only unpleasantness in the *Sublime Porte*.

The Austrian steamship, which went from Constantinople over the

Black Sea to connect with the steamers going up the Danube, was due to leave in the next few days. This journey interested me very much because it would give me the opportunity to see a great part of Bulgaria, Wallachia, Serbia and Hungary. But there was unrest in Rumelia[1] and fear that the troubles might spread to the neighboring countries. For three whole weeks now the Austrian mail (which goes via Belgrade to Constantinople) had not arrived, and everyone was convinced that the courier had been murdered or imprisoned. No one knew anything for certain and no security measures were being taken. The Austrian and Russian Ministers had sent couriers to Adrianople and the Balkans, but the information they had obtained was very incomplete. All that was certain was that the harshness and injustice of the Turkish tax-collectors had brought the Christian families in the cities of Nissa and Sofia to the point of revolt. During the Greek Easter, the Turks were reported to have entered the churches and to have attacked women and children. Over two thousand were said to have been murdered.

Every ten days one can make the journey from Constantinople over the Black Sea and up the Danube to Vienna; but as the situation now was there was fear that the longer journey would be postponed. Indeed it was becoming more and more uncertain that it could be done at all—in which case I should have to go back via Greece and Italy. In the hotel where I was staying were two Frenchmen and an Englishman; we had agreed to do the Danube trip to Vienna together. But now they simply gave up and decided to make their way home through Italy. They now regarded the Danube journey as a completely stupid project; they were, they said, strengthened in this opinion by all the authorities. They thought it very unlikely indeed that the Bulgarian rebels would respect the Austrian flag, and even if one were not killed then one would certainly be exposed to continued unpleasantness and discomfort.

I confess that I had a very restless, painful night before I could make

---

[1] As Andersen began his trip up the Danube, he found this part of Europe still largely controlled by the Ottoman Empire. Bulgaria was ruled by Turks, as were Wallachia and Moldavia (to the north of the Danube) and Rumelia (to the south)—now all part of Rumania. Serbia had won its independence in 1817. Hungary was part of the Austro-Hungarian Empire.

up my mind. If I wanted to go with that ship then I had to embark the very next evening. On the one hand, fear of the many dangers which, by all accounts, were in store and, on the other, my burning desire to see and experience something new and interesting—the conflict set fever in my blood.

Early in the morning I went to Baron Stürmer, told him the problem, and asked for his advice.[2] He said that a Russian courier had arrived the previous evening, having passed through the very district that we should have to go through to get to the Danube from the Black Sea; he had found no signs of disturbance there yet. Further he said that two Austrian officers, Colonel Philippovich and Major Tratner, both of whom were returning home from campaigns in Syria and whom I had met at dinners here in this house, were due to take the Danube journey home by the ship which was leaving early the next morning. Since the courier could not go, all the dispatches and letters—together with a considerable sum of money—were being handed over to Philippovich, who could claim and expect every protection in even the worst circumstances. I could attach myself to these two gentlemen.

The journey was therefore now decided and from that moment all my fears vanished. That same hour news was received in Pera which, for the moment, superseded the main topic of conversation—about unrest in the country. It was the sad news that the steamship *Stambul*, the biggest ship owned by the Austrian Company, had that morning under the heavy fogs that roll over the Black Sea crashed against a rock twelve miles east of *Amastra* and was completely wrecked—but all the passengers were saved.

May 5, 1841

Towards evening I left Pera. From the cemetery under the high round tower my eyes drank in once again the vast and wonderful panorama of Constantinople, the Sea of Marmora and snow-capped Olympus.

---

[2] Baron Bartholomaus von Stürmer (1787–1863) was the Austrian Internuntius and Minister Plenipotentiary in Constantinople. Andersen was introduced to him by Prokesch-Osten, the Austrian minister in Athens. The section of this book called "The Orient" is dedicated in part to Baron von Stürmer.

The steamship *Ferdinando I* was to carry me over *Pontus Euxinus:*[3] it was comfortable and good on board; in the first class, in addition to Philippovich, Tratner and me, there was only one other passenger, an Englishman called Ainsworth,[4] who had been sent out on an expedition to Kurdistan and had lately come from Babylon.

On board I found a whole flock of deck passengers: Turks, Jews, Bulgars and Wallachians, who made themselves very comfortable, boiled their coffee and stretched out to sleep. Boats cruised around our vessel, ships came and went. There was life on the water and a humming and shouting from within Pera and Constantinople as if there were riot in the streets. Only Naples can give one any idea of what it was like.

Over the dark cypresses of the seraglio garden the moon stood, round and full, but quite pale in the light blue air. The sun went down; its red rays fell on the windows over in Scutari—it looked just as if one bonfire after another were being lit. It dazzled the eye—and then, in a moment, the light was put out; darkness glided over the clear water, over the domes and minarets. Dolphins sported close by our ship. From beside the seraglio gondolas sped over the Bay; they were rowed by ten or twelve oarsmen, all with wide-winged sleeves which hung down, leaving their strong arms bare. They all kept to a quick measured rhythm. A gondola flew by, arrow-swift, and in the stern, on high colored cushions and rich carpets which hung over the water, sat a grave Turk, his arms crossed—it was like a dream vision, a scene in a fairy tale. The stars twinkled and down from the minarets came the deep monotone cry of the Muezzin, telling the hour.

---

[3] Pontus Euxinus is the ancient name for the Black Sea. It means "hospitable sea." Ancient Greeks colonized its shores as early as the 8th century B.C.

[4] William Francis Ainsworth (1807–1896) was a doctor, geologist and traveler who published his *Journey to Angora* in 1838. He and Andersen shared accommodation in quarantine, and clearly got on well together. In an article in *The Literary Gazette* in 1846, Ainsworth described Andersen as "friendly and cheerful in conversation, although restless and pre-occupé." He mentioned Andersen's skill in cutting out paper and apparently used Andersen's cutting of the whirling dervishes in his book of his travels in Asia.

The Bosphorus

May 5 and 6, 1841

The Bosphorus is like a river with the transparency, the clearness of the sea, a salt-water river that joins the oceans—a river between two parts of the world, where every spot is picturesque, every place historic: here the Orient pays court to Europe and dreams of being the master. I know of no other stretch like this, where strength and greatness are united as here. Even the banks of the Rhine in their autumn beauty do not have the color of the shores of the Bosphorus. The Rhine seems narrow compared with these glass-green waters, and yet I was reminded of the Rhine and of Mälaren between Stockholm and Uppsala, when the warm summer sun shines between the dark pines and the shimmering birch trees.

In most places the water is not so broad that one cannot clearly see everything on both coasts. It twists and turns in seven bends over a three-mile long course between the Sea of Marmora and the Black Sea, and for practically the whole length the European coast looks like one city, one single street, behind which the mountains rise up —not very grand but always large enough to be called mountains, and on them there flourishes a garden, a real botanical garden. Here are birch trees as in Sweden and Norway, groups of beeches as in Denmark, pines, plane trees and chestnuts as we see them in Italy and cypresses, tall and strong as only the grave-yards in Pera and Scutari can produce. And in the midst of this luxuriant green rises the palm with its broad crown, a memorial column that tells us where we really are in the world.

If we turn our eyes to the Asiatic side, it is just as rich, just as varied, only not with the mass of buildings that give us the impression that the European coast is one continuous city. Here, on the other side, the plains are greater, the mountains are higher and more free-ranging.

I was to spend the fifth of May, the anniversary of the death of Napoleon, on the Black Sea. There are more spiritual feast-days for each of us than are marked in the almanac as Sundays and Holy days. The history of the world and of our own life marks out individual days that do not appear of note in the calendar. In remembering some special event I have often felt very strongly how prosaic and empty that particular day had been for me; but this year one of the famous days of the present age was indeed very special and festive for me: that morning at half-past four I would sail from Constantinople through the Bosphorus and out into the Black Sea.

Topschana and Pera seemed to be part of Constantinople, with Scutari as a suburb. With its white minarets, red-brown houses and green gardens, Scutari now lay in clear sunshine, which streamed over the whole of the Asiatic coast. One could see the charming high-lying village of Kandelli, the Imperial garden and the vast palaces of the nobles. What richness, what natural beauty there was around the coasts of the Bosphorus!

When I was a boy, how often did my thoughts sail through "A thousand and one nights"—and I saw fantastic castles of marble, with hanging gardens and cool, springing waters. Here such a picture came before me in reality, brought to life in every detail—for on the European side was the newly finished summer palace in which, last year, Abdul Meschid had been the first Sultan to live. It is in eastern style and very large, with marble columns and high terraces.

The palace gardens stretch down to the village of Kurutscheme whose peculiar wooden buildings along the water-front attract attention. One story overhangs the other, supported by slanting timbers. The ground floor is in this way as good as covered over by the upper, protecting story. A number of elderly *Sultanas* live here, and the windows are therefore well latticed outside with shutters—which naturally are not without their spy-holes, through which the once beautiful and powerful can look out to the water and the foreign ships. . . . .

Our ship began to rock and the mate explained that the strongest currents in the Bosphorus were found here.

The lovely valley of Bebek with its pleasure-palace opened out before us, bordered by the dark cypresses of a graveyard. These few words are inadequate—the eye must see this valley which, like an English park in bright sunshine, shows a variety of green that is not blended on any palette. One must see these poplars, whose shimmering branches seem to play with their shadow on the ground; it is these groups of leafy trees under whose shady roof the wild turtledove has his seraglio; these fat green grassy plains where the shiny white oxen stand like ancient marble sculptures, half hidden in the tall grass. Here is life, sunshine and pleasure and close by lies the border, the dark cypress wood, with death, shadow and peace.

We glided past the cemetery; picturesque cliffs rose up; we were at the place where Androcles from Samos threw the bridge over the Bosphorus, across which Darius led the Persians into Europe against the Scythians. One of the rocks here was cut into a throne for Darius, from which he could see the passage. No trace of this remains. Ottoman saints rest at the foot of the rock, the ground the savage armies once trod is now sacred; tall dark cypresses stand guard over the graves. The fleeing birds of the Bosphorus, which sailors call "lost souls," flew at us and turned again in the same instant. On the Asiatic and European sides lie the great fortresses of Anatoli, Hissari and Rumeli Hissari—they were intended to guard the entrance, but the gun emplacements have been walled up and the buildings have long since turned into prisons; the castles are now called "the black towers" and in them thousands of Christians have languished.

It is more beautiful here on the Asiatic side.

Between lime trees, weeping willow and plane trees, *Sultanje* rises up like an amphitheater and is reflected upside down in the still surface of the coastal waters. The slender white minaret which, in reality, points up to heaven and the one that points downward in the water seem to say—do not look at life only in the sunshine around you, see it too in the moving waters between two parts of the world. And in truth there was life and movement. Large boats, with Turkish women swathed in white airy veils, crossed from one coast to the other. Long fishing boats shot past the great ships which came from the Black Sea, the double eagle of Russia spreading its wings on the proud flags. Rocking gently on the waters by a fishing village—I think it was Baikos—lay some huts with nets attached in which the swordfish would be caught: I say huts, but one could also call them baskets, in each of which sat a half-naked fisherman looking after the catch.

On the European side we drew near to Therapia, in whose deep bay lay a couple of great ships. A little boat met us here with an old Negro at the oar. He had on a woolen smock like the Greeks wear. The boat was, quite literally, filled with roses. A little Greek girl, with her dark hair plaited about her red fez and a large gold coin entwined in it, stood up leaning against one of the baskets of roses; in her hand she had one of those Bulgarian hand-drums. The boat rocked with the increased movement of the waves; the strong speed of our ship raised the current, and the little girl held closer to one of the baskets which fell over with her and tipped its stream of roses over her chest and face. She got up again and when she saw that we were looking at her she laughed, struck her little drum and then threw it into the basket, holding a handful of roses in front of her face. The boat, the Negro and the little girl and, as background, Therapia with its gardens, buildings and ships—this was a picture that deserved to be recorded.

A bigger and broader bay than we had seen before was the foreground for my next picture. The summer residence of the Ambassadors, "Bujukderek," lay before us. Among the flags of many different nations which were flying there, I looked for that of my fatherland—and I found it! I saw the white cross on the red ground: Denmark had planted its white cross of Christ in the land of the Turk. The flag fluttered in the wind—it was as though it brought me a greeting from home. My neighbor at the ship's rail pointed out the great aqueduct with its double arches, rising up in the green of the deep valley. Another passenger spoke of Medea, who had wandered here where now the seamen pulled up their boats under the tall plane trees, but I had eyes and thoughts only for the Danish flag which I saw for the first time during my whole journey. . . .

The beauty and gentleness of the Bosphorus was suddenly transformed—and here was nature in the wild. Yellowish lacerated rocks rose up out of the water. Batteries, intended to protect the Bosphorus against the inroads of the Cossacks, heightened the harshness of the view. The tower higher up is called Ovid's Tower and legend has it— but falsely—that it was here that the poet sat as a prisoner by the Black Sea. The tower is now a ruin; it is used as a lighthouse; when the sun is down great torches are lit up there and the red flames light the way for the ships of the Black Sea.

There is a short stretch of green again on the Asiatic side but soon, where the coasts are very near to each other, wild mountain country appears boldly on both sides. In Asia the mountain range of Bythynia ends here, in Europe, the Thracian. No paths now twist along the shore; the mountain goats clamber high on the strange cliffs. The Black Sea lies open before us and on the point of two continents of the world lie lighthouses—with welcome lights or goodbye stars, according to which course the ship is steering.

Near to the coast, curious rock islands rise up—they seem to be thrown one against the other, with one block of stone holding fast to the next. The story goes that these mountains were once floating— they crushed ships between them—and only when the Argonauts succeeded in sailing past were they bound fast.

The sun shone on the bare stones, the sea lay endlessly vast before us and we sailed ahead. The mists, which during the whole of our passage through the Bosphorus rose and sank but never quite hid the coasts, now closed in like a curtain coming down on a splendid opera set. In an instant the coasts of Asia and Europe were hidden from us. The sea-birds formed a ring round the ship's funnel and I looked back again—we could see only sea and mist.

The Black Sea

While we were sailing through the Bosphorus we had eyes only for the lovely panorama of the landscape—and now this was finished. We seemed to be skimming through clouds which moved over the sea more quickly than we were doing. There was something so northern and familiar in these mists, that for me it was as though I were sailing on the Kattegat in November. One had to wrap up in all the winter clothes one had and the farther we went the colder it got. The clammy fog oppressed us for half an hour and then, in a flash, it was gone. The sun shone clear and the air was a lovely blue, although the water did not have the blueness and transparency of the Mediterranean. The Black Sea has almost the character of our northern seas—with short waves, close and dull in color, leaden, in contrast with the light shining waters of the Mediterranean.

Our ship, cutting through the waters here where once the Argonauts sailed, was neither in size nor comforts a steamer of the first grade. And yet, in the time of Jason, it would have been reckoned as more than royal—indeed it would have been labeled as a work of magic. Soft divans and commodious cabins were set round a large decorative saloon, with mirrors, pictures and books. On the table were fresh Egyptian figs, picked a week ago; there were grapes from Smyrna, wine from faraway Gaul. But the most magical thing, the great spark, the flaming monster which carried the ship against currents and winds, lay inside the vessel and sent out from there its breath, its pulse, like coal-black smoke, a cloud which lay over the sea. Medea could not have created the like; the discoveries of our time are greater than the greatest magic of bygone centuries. Genius no longer belongs to the individual—it belongs to the whole world.

Now in clear sunshine, now swathed in fog, we go on our way. In addition to the four passengers I have named before in the first class, there was in the second and third class another little group coming with us to Vienna. The most conspicuous was Peter Adam, an Armenian priest, in black habit, with a hat the size of a knight's shield. He had not seen his friends in the imperial city of the Danube for twenty-five years and he was now traveling there for a short visit as the escort of two Armenian boys, the nephews of the Armenian Bishop. The elder, Hieronimus, with a round girlish face, was to study medicine; the younger, Antonio Maruz, particularly handsome, with wise expressive eyes and a personal pride in every movement, intended to be a priest. Both wore the fez on their heads and slippers on their feet. The farewell to their home was already forgotten; the elder boy stretched himself out and smoked his cigar, the younger looked at some holy pictures. A young fat Jew who tried to meddle in everything, a good-natured young waiter and a sea-sick chamber-maid (who was always in her berth so that we had not yet seen her), three Germans, a young Turk and two Greeks were the rest of the company who were going to make the whole journey with us. The others were only going as far as Kustendje and Silistra.

Just as in the Mediterranean we also got a weary flying passenger here—a little bird came to rest on the deck, ate some bread-crumbs and drank water from a saucer. Towards evening he flew away from us, straight towards the East. I bade it greet the Caucasian mountains, to greet the wild scrubland by the rivers where the tiger slakes his thirst, to greet the city of Tiflis and the charming Circassian women. I wanted so much to see everything in the East. But this time, at least, it would not happen; we were steering towards the North, the damp, stormy way; the stars twinkled, as lovely as over Greece and the Mediterranean, but here it was cold. One would think we were making a summer expedition to Spitsbergen and not sailing on the Black Sea in the month of May.

During the night I awoke at the sound of casting anchor. The fog was so thick that the captain, thinking of the stranding of the *Stambul*, dared not sail further. (In winter and spring it is very dangerous indeed to sail over this stretch of the Black Sea between the Bosphorus and Odessa. Many ships are lost; last winter two ships were wrecked.) At dawn it cleared a little and we sailed again, but after a few minutes we had to lay by again. It was as though a thick steam poured out of the sea; there were great drops of water on the deck and gunwale, the rigging was wet as if it had been at the bottom of the sea.

Then in a moment the sun broke through, the coast appeared, low and uninhabited—it was the district of Dobrudscha; there was not a house, not a tree, not a buoy to be seen; but from the flat contour of the land the Captain reckoned that we had come about two miles farther north than we should have done. The vessel was soon turned around and we went over the foaming green waves towards a little bay. The anchor fell and now for the first time the sick stewardess appeared, with a smile at the coast, which did not smile back. Good-bye, sea of the Argonauts! Over your waters I take from the Orient, if not the Golden Fleece of Poetry, at least its memory!

Journey Over the Steppes Between the Black Sea and the Danube

May 7, 1841, Romania

Constanza, Romania offers a low coastline, the slopes of which are chalky earth pitted with shells. There was not a tree or bush to be seen—just a few windowless huts with thatched roofs right down to the ground surrounded by stone hedges. A flag waved; a group of heavily veiled women observed our arrival.

Through strong breakers our boat reached land, where some screaming Tartars received us.

The landing-stage consisted of some fallen blocks of stone between which, in order to even them out a little, bits of sod had been thrown. The wooden huts seemed to have been erected in great haste; the whole coast was like a desert where only yesterday or today some dwellings had been thrown up. Our baggage was piled into a couple of wagons drawn by oxen and taken off to the inn. The inn was really quite impressive in these surroundings, and its cleanliness was particularly inviting. A balcony with a thatched roof led to the best room where the first class passengers were quartered.

While a meal was being prepared we went for a walk through the town.

In 1809 Constanza was completely destroyed by the Russians and everything here looked as if this destruction had happened only a few weeks ago. Half ruined houses made up the main street, which was fairly broad. Here and there lay columns of marble and granite that seemed to belong to an older time. On some of the houses the roof or the upper projecting story was supported by a wooden plank which rested on an antique marble capital. The minaret of the town's one and only—and half tumbledown—mosque was built of timbers and chalked white. There was of course a café, but its appearance was, like that of its customers, extremely wretched. Here on the projecting balcony lay some Turks; they smoked their pipes, drank their coffee and seemed to take no notice of us foreigners.

A couple of dreadfully ragged men with long beards, caftans, turbans and leather slippers, went along the street, gathering dung for fuel, because there are no trees here for many miles around.

Close by the town there were not insignificant remains of Trajan's walls, which are said to have stretched from the Black Sea here to the Danube. So far as the eye could see, all around there was only the sea or the endless steppe, not a house, no smoke from a shepherd's bonfire, no herds of cattle, no sign of life. There was just an unending green plain. Near to the town there were a few patches, not enclosed or hedged, where corn was growing—no higher than grass and with the same color.

I wandered down to the sea; close by, right under a slope, the first thing my eye fell upon was a dead stork. It lay, with one wing out-stretched, its neck bowed. I felt quite sad at the sight—the stork has always been one of the most interesting birds for me; it filled my thoughts when I was a child, it haunts my novels and stories,[1] and now it was the first thing I saw at the moment when I turned home-wards over the sea. It had just managed to reach these shores—and then had died. I had a superstitious thought—and surely no one can say that in the whole of his life he has been absolutely without such an idea—that perhaps I too should have managed to cross the sea—and then that would be the end of my life.

While I was looking at the bird, the damp fog rolled in again over the sea and coast, so thick and close that for a moment I was afraid that I should not be able to find my way back to the inn. I could not see four steps in front of me, but I went straight on, clambered over a stone fence and so came to another but shorter way to the inn,

---

[1] Andersen's story of *The Storks* is based on common superstitions and nursery rhymes. Later stories involving storks were *The Marsh King's Daughter* of 1858 and *The Toad* of 1866. One of the still current nursery songs in Denmark is *The Stork on the Farmer's Roof* which is indeed one of the magic sights of a Danish summer.

where an excellent meal was waiting—so well prepared indeed that even if all my readers were to say, "Must we now hear about food?" it would not matter—they must hear it—FOOD. It was first class and, as we learned the next day, unbelievably cheap. None of us had experienced such a thing before. We wrote down the names of the host and hostess and promised to spread their fame abroad; I will do it here and say that the man is an Austrian, Thomas Radicsevitch and that he lives on the corner of the Black Sea.

After the meal our baggage was packed into great wooden wagons which would now go to the Danube, and since they were drawn by oxen they would take the whole afternoon, evening and night and the following day to reach Czernawoda. We therefore were to spend the night in Constanza and would then, by leaving early in the morning, get there at the same time as our trunks. Wallachian peasants, dressed in sheepskin cloaks and black felt hats, whose monstrous brims hung down literally like umbrellas over their backs and chests, accompanied the wagons. We were assured that this stretch of country was completely peaceful and that on our steppe journey we would not meet other than Wallachian nomads.

A thick damp mist again rolled in from the sea over the whole district; the laden wagons drove off and disappeared as in a cloud a few steps away from us. It was as cold as out on the open sea.

The host told us about these strong and quick changes in temperature and weather, about last winter's fearful storms and about the cold. There had been ice several miles out to sea and one could drive over it from Constanza down to Varna. He told us about the snowstorm which drove the shepherds with their herds across the steppes, and about the stray dogs of which we saw a number. Through the whole of Bulgaria and Rumelia, especially during winter, these howling packs pass through. They often meet up with wolves and the attack is equally savage on both sides. A single vixen who goes off with the dogs is often accepted by them; the young she produces are indistinguishable from those of her own kind and she suckles them with care. But when they are a few days old she carries them down to the river and if they then lap the water with their tongues in the manner of the dog—then she tears them to pieces. Instinct tells her that they are the worst enemies of her own race.

Towards evening the weather was fine. I walked along the shore with Ainsworth in order to collect some stones and shells. We passed the dead stork and close by it lay another wretched dead animal, which I must have seen before but had really taken no notice of—and yet it was perhaps more interesting than the stork. It was a large poodle, presumably thrown overboard from a ship and now washed up here on land. One could write a sea and an air romance about these two. We do not have air romances yet, but they will certainly come—with the Balloons!

On the way back we visited one of those wretched Tartar huts with the thatch going down to the ground; in fact we crawled into the room, which looked like a vast chimney. The walls were covered with soot and everything above us was lost in smoke. An unveiled Tartar girl stood by the fire cooking meat on a stick. Beautiful she certainly was not; her features were very coarse, her eyes too light-blue, but in her figure and posture a painter could have found a subject for a very distinctive picture, with double illumination—the fire within the hut and the evening sun which shone in blood-red through the low door.

At the inn a bowl of punch was steaming on the table. We spent a pleasant cheerful evening; German entertainment, the German language and comfort almost led us to believe that, in an instant, we had flown from the Orient into the middle of Germany.

Along the walls under the windows—all around the room—there were broad divans with straw-mats: these were our couches. I could not sleep. The surf sounded like thunder; through the window I could see the broad sea lit up by the clear round moon.

We were due to leave early the next morning. Peasants came with pleasant Wallachian horses, which danced outside our door. Two got loose and leaped over the stone enclosure, kicking out with their back legs. Everyone started yelling and shouting and I took myself down to the sea, to say goodbye; the open salt sea that I love so much I should now not see again until I reached Denmark.

At last our procession was in order. Our host, in his old Austrian uniform, rode first and we others followed at a brisk pace through the town and out on to the open, endless steppe. To the left, for the whole of our day's journey, stretched the Kurasu lake, which is said to be the remains of the canal by which Trajan linked the Danube and the Black Sea. It could easily be put into use again, but it would certainly be less expensive on this even ground to lay down a railway. The only difficulty in the execution of such a project would probably be objections from the Turkish side. It was apparently difficult enough for the Danube-Steamship Company to get permission to build inns and offices here so that their travelers could take the shorter way through the country. I was told that the license was restricted to the Austrian Danube-Steamship Committee, their families and friends.

We passed some entrenchments from the last Russian war. They had been quite undermined by wild dogs, who find coolness in these holes in summer when the sun burns down on the shadowless steppe, and shelter in winter when storm and snow beat down on their heads.

At last we reached a village, where every house looked like a dung-heap on a stone cairn. To the right there were a couple of granite columns from a ruined monastery.

We passed on and only the green, lonely steppe stretched out before us and to all sides. Three Turks with turbans and flowing colored caftans, came towards us at full tilt. "Allah Akbar" was their greeting.

In the middle of the silent steppe lay an abandoned Turkish grave-yard with white, broken grave-stones; only on a few was the engraved turban still visible. Not a cypress, not a bush, cast its shadow over the dead; the village which had lain there had been wiped off the face of the earth.

In this uniform, monotonous flatness even the most insignificant object that stood out attracted our attention. A large eagle sat in the grass and did not leave his place until we were only about fifty paces away. We saw herds of cattle, which at a distance looked like armies in battle formation. The Wallachian herdsmen looked exactly like savages. They wore long sheepskin coats with the wool turned outside and monstrous large hats or narrow caps of shaggy skin; long stiff black hair hung down over their shoulders. All of them carried heavy axes. The sun burned as I have never felt it before. The heat poured over us and we almost fainted from thirst. Most people spread their hand-kerchiefs over some small pools of water which swarmed with insects—and then sucked up the water. I could only manage to wet my lips; and in this burning sun and heat the Wallachian shepherds stood in their heavy skin cloaks, leaning on their axes. . . .

Wretched nomads! We rush past them. A little khan, put up for travelers, was inviting: coffee was heated and the food we had brought with us was eaten; we were ourselves both guests and hosts. No one lived there; the doors and windows were locked again when we had rested and we were on our way once more with renewed strength and speed—forward in the same direction as before. The countryside be-came less flat and, like a green sea out towards the horizon, grassy Wallachia appeared.

We passed low hills with leafy trees, beeches and birches—it was all very Danish, so gentle and smiling. And now we were in Czer-nawoda, a splendid example of a decayed town, with its own kind of picturesque beauty; one house seemed to strive to outdo the next. On one the roof consisted only of three or four timbers on which there hung a wisp of thatch while another house was nothing but roof, which went right down to the ground. A crowd of children poured out from every door—or rather hole; most of the little ones were completely naked, one indeed did have a sheepskin cap on his head, but that was all. A boy had his father's great caftan around him, but it was open and one could see that he wore nothing else.

The Danube had risen high up over the fields, its waters splashing under our horses' feet. From the steamship *Argo* the Austrian flag flew, waving to us as a home. Inside was a saloon with mirrors, books, a map and divans; the table was laid ready with warm food, fruit and wine. Everything was good; all was well on board.

Part Four

JOURNEY UP THE DANUBE

From Czernawoda to Rustchuk

May 8 and 9, 1841

It was three o'clock in the afternoon when our Danube trip began.[1] The crew was Italian. All of us on board soon got very fond of the Captain, Marco Dobroslawich, a Dalmatian, a humorous, excellent old man. He ran rough-shod over the sailors, but all the same they really loved him and actually looked as if they were enjoying it when he berated them, because he was always ready with a good word, which made up for the scolding. During the nights and days it took us to reach the military border none was more active and in better temper than our old Captain. In the middle of the night when we could still sail, one heard his commanding voice, always in the same spirits, always ready with a box on the ear and a cheerful word and at the dinner table he was a jovial, good-natured host. He was certainly the pearl among all the Danube captains. As we went on, the other captains were progressively less friendly and one felt progressively less at home and less comfortable. Naturally, among strangers and strange customs we all drew closer together although, as we got nearer to Pest and Vienna, there were so many passengers on board that people kept themselves to themselves. But with Father Marco it was just like being in a "pension."

The whole of the afternoon sailing from Czernawoda was between

[1] Every fourteen days one can go with Austrian steamships from Constantinople over the Black Sea and up the Danube to Vienna. There are two different routes: the one is from the Black Sea through the mouth of the Danube to Galatz, where there is 7 days' quarantine—then one sails along the Wallachian coast, which is quite flat and has few towns, to Orsova, where there is another but shorter period of quarantine. The other route, which I chose, is far more interesting; one does not go up to the mouth of the Danube but lands at Kustendje and then goes over land, a whole day's journey, to the Danube at the town of Czernawoda. This way the river trip is shortened by 3 days. Further there is the advantage that the boat keeps to the left side going up-river where the countryside is more varied, and one can go ashore in a number of the larger Bulgarian towns and can take walks in the Serbian forests. In Orsova one gets the quarantine period over in one go—it lasts for 10 days; after that the journey continues to Pest and from there to Vienna. HCA.

flooded islands, with the tops of willow trees and the gables of thatched huts sticking up out of the water. Nowhere yet could we see the whole breadth of the Danube. We passed a happy evening in the beautiful, well-lit cabin. The rye-bread taste in the real Tokay reminded me of the country of rye—faraway Denmark. But the night was not like the evening! In these marshy regions the heat of summer hatches out not only fevers but also millions of poisonous midges, which plague the inhabitants of the region and the crews of the riverboats in the most frightful way. Untold hordes of gnats had hatched out these last nights and they swarmed in at us through the open shutters. No one had expected their coming yet; they fell upon us and jabbed so that the blood ran down over our faces and hands.

Early in the morning, before even the sun was up, we were all on deck—each one of us with bleeding and swollen face. Around midnight we had passed the Turkish fortress of Silistra and had taken some Turkish deck passengers on board. They lay swathed in great blankets and slept among the sacks of coal.

Now it was daylight. The Danube islands stood under water; they looked like swimming forests which were on the point of sinking. The view on the Wallachian side was of an endless green plain, on which the only variation was a tumble-down guardhouse made of clay and straw, or a rectangular white-washed quarantine building with a red roof. There was no garden and not a single tree; the building lay isolated like the ship of the Flying Dutchman on an untraveled, dead-still sea. The Bulgarian side, on the other hand, was covered with bushes and thickets and the rich soil seemed to be specially suitable for cultivation. But long stretches lay completely at waste. Thousands of people emigrate from Europe to America; surely they could far better find a home and fertile fields here, close by Europe's greatest river, the highway to the Orient.

On the Bulgarian side we were greeted by the first town, Tutrakan; in front of each house there was a little garden, and half-naked boys ran along the sloping bank and shouted *Urolah*. Everything here looked peaceful still, with no sign of danger. The unrest within the country had not yet reached these shores. But we heard from the Turks who had come on board last night at Silistra that a number of refugees had crossed the Danube there to seek refuge in Bucharest. On that side of the mountains revolt was raging—and death.

About Tutrakan we passed a very picturesque gorge; luxuriant hedges hung out over the high slopes of red-brown earth. A flock of lovely black horses was being driven down to cross the river—one of them distinguished itself partly by its lively behavior, partly by its coal-black color and long flowing mane. It leaped about so that the earth spurted under its hooves.

The next settlement we reached on the Bulgarian side was Havai. Wild roses bloomed there in the warm sunshine; hedges, trees and houses were grouped around the white minaret in a very lovely setting. A writer of romance could indeed have used this as the background for a story—and in fact Havai does offer the material for such a story, and it is historical. The late Sultan Mahmud,[2] father of Abdul-Mesched, once made a journey on the Danube; there was a terrible storm and the vessel was near to sinking. At Havai the Ruler of the Faithful went ashore and spent the night here. Whether he slept well and had pleasant dreams I do not know, but for the inhabitants of Havai that night is a beautiful, vanished dream. . . .

Not far from here we saw the first water mills. They lay on fast-tethered river boats and when winter comes they are pulled up on land in the lee of the bushes. The family then sit inside the silent mill, with only the hand-drum and the flute for entertainment; the music is as monotonous as that of the cricket. The family is bored with life on land and longs for spring, so that the mill can rock on the rushing stream, the wheels turning and life moving again. They stand in their parlor door and fish, while the steamers travel by.

The sun was burning hot: our awning gave some shade but the air was heated through as in an oven and the temperature increased. Nothing refreshed the body, nothing refreshed the soul. Around us

---

[2] Mahmud II (1785–1839) was the sultan who put down an uprising of the Greeks in 1821, and suppressed the Janissaries in 1826. In 1833 he made a treaty with the Russians, in an effort to suppress Mehemet Ali in Egypt. He died in 1839, before learning of the defeat of his armies by Mehemet Ali. He was succeeded by his young son, Abdul Mesched.

was always the same green, an endless idyll; it was as though we were sailing between asparagus tips and parsley. The heat became more and more oppressive; we felt as if we were in a steam bath, but there was no cooling shower and there was not a cloud in the sky. Such a degree of warmth I have never imagined in my chill fatherland.

At last we saw a town on the Wallachian side; it was Giurgiu whose defense works had been destroyed by the Russians. From here it is only six hours' journey to Bucharest, the capital of Wallachia. From here some of the townsfolk had assembled on the ramparts; there was a lot of shouting and questions about health conditions in Constantinople and about the unrest in the interior of the country.[3] The sun went down at that moment; the town's church tower which had newly been covered with shining tin plates, now shone like silver and hurt one's eyes. The air was summerlike over the flat green meadows. Marsh birds flew up from the reeds. On the Bulgarian side yellow cliffs rose up; we steered in under them and while we could still see the shining tower of Giurgiu we were alongside the houses and gardens on the outskirts of Rustchuk[4]—a fairly large Bulgarian town. A mass of minarets, one close to the other, showed that it must be a city of genuine believers. The whole quay and landing stage were crowded with people, who were making a remarkable commotion. We were close by the jetty when, amid a dreadful screaming, two men in Frankish dress but wearing the fez fell into the water. They both swam towards land; one was helped out, but the other was driven back—with stones thrown after him. He turned towards our ship and shouted to us in French, "Help! They'll murder me!" A couple of our sailors jumped into a boat and fished him up. Our vessel turned off again from land and all the passengers and crew flocked to the railing. Perhaps the difficulties of our travel through a land in revolt had begun! What *was* happening in Rustchuk? There followed a few uncertain, anxious moments. Some signals were given and answered. Soldiers appeared

---

[3] For the moment there was no plague but it was raging in Alexandria and Cairo. From a letter I received during my last days in Pera, I heard that in both places several hundred people were dying each day. HCA.
[4] Now Ruse, Bulgaria

on the bridge and a boat was rowed out to us with Hephys,[5] the minor Pascha of the town on board. He was escorted onto our ship by two of his officers. The way this was done was very peculiar; one held him by each wrist, the other took him by the elbow and shoulder—and thus they moved forward to the Captain's cabin, where they were entertained with preserves and liqueurs. Later he inspected the various cabins, escorted the same way as when he arrived, except that two young Turks carried burning tapers before him.

As to the tumult, it turned out to be a private quarrel. The two opposing parties were the Quarantine Director, a Turk, and the doctor, a Frenchman. They were always quarreling and when this happened yet again, but this time at the landing—they pushed each other over—and the Turks took the Turk's part.

Meanwhile on board the doctor was given dry clothing and, under the protection of the Pascha, left our vessel which now lay against the jetty. The soldiers had cleared it of the crowd. We were taking coal in; it was now evening and dark. Only one lamp shone in the rigging. All was quiet in Rustchuk. A stray dog howled, the Muezzin called the hours from the minaret, a solitary light wavered through the black, lonely streets.

Our beds were hung around with green gauze, so that we could be protected from the swarms of poisonous gnats. My companions sat themselves down in the meantime to play cards. I do not know a single game. The map of the Danube was my "hand," and I studied this, the imperishable highway to the Orient which, year by year, will become more and more traveled and soon on its mighty stream will bear poets who know how to mine the treasure of poetry that lies in every bush and beneath every stone. . . .

---

[5] In Rustchuk (Ruse) there are no less than 3 Paschas—the most important is Mersa Said, the next is Mohammed and the third is Hephys. HCA.

We Sail!

It is a beautiful morning. With the broad open green plains, the smell of hay—are we in Denmark? Just look at the mass of flowers, the grass-grown hillocks, the small mounds made by the hand of man—just as in parts of Denmark. It is all very idyllic, just like a Danish summer and yet we are not in Denmark. The green fields smelling of hay are Wallachian; the barrows to the left are in Bulgaria. Close by the river bank lies a hut—just some straw matting hung over a couple of poles. The shepherd's family sits outside, their great dog barks at the sight and sound of our vessel.

There are new faces on board; during the night Rustchuk sent us a lot of guests, and what a motley group they are too. The Turk kneels and says his morning prayer, his forehead touching the deck. Hard by sits a Jew in a silver-gray robe with purple colored turban; his yellow slippers lie in front of him. He holds an umbrella over himself, although the sun is not shining on him. He takes a little hand-mirror, looks at himself in it, smiles and now and again tweaks a gray hair out of his beard with a small pair of tweezers.

We fly past the Bulgarian towns. What is that one called? It is Vardin—when I hear the nightingale singing among the flowering wild lilacs I shall remember its sisters in this spot. Another town—this is Sistowa. High over it rise the walls of a fortress. Turks with long pipes recline on the wooden balconies of the houses and look with total indifference at our steamship's speed—just as they look at the smoke from their pipes. Now a town on the right, a Wallachian town with wretched mud huts and a long deathly still quarantine building. It is Simnitza. We write down your name—and then forget you!

Something is shining in front of us—how white the slopes are on the Bulgarian side; they got clearer and clearer. But this is Danish—they are surely the white cliffs of Møen that rise up to meet me. I know all the shapes, I recognize the summer green high up on the white slopes. But these are only bushes—Møen has woods, beneath it Møen has the clear blue-green sea and not these muddy brown waves of the Danube. A town lies up there—it is Nicopolis, Trajan's city,[1] the trophy of Bajazet. We glide close under the white slopes; the skipper points at a row of deep holes in the cliff side; they look like great embrasures in the wall of a fortress. They are ancient graves. Who were the heroes and princes who became dust here, while the yellow river, unchanging, casts it waves against the rocky ground? No one knows and now the swallows nest in the grave chambers of heroes. . . .

Between the white cliffs and the green plains of Wallachia a lovely rainbow stands high over the river, whose waves ripple as on an inland lake. If only I were a painter. . . .

On the Balkan mountains the white snow caps glow in the setting sun. The Turk kneels, he bows his head to the ground and mumbles his evening prayer. The sun is down, there is peace in nature and in my heart. We sail on through the clear night. . . .

---

[1] Nicopolis was conquered by the Emperor Trajan, who ruled from 98 to 117 A.D. The area became the Roman colony called Dacia. King Sigismund of Hungary was defeated at Nicopolis in 1396 by the Turks under Bajazet I (1347–1403).

Unquiet Journey

It was the middle of the night. We were all awakened when the ship suddenly stopped still. We could hear loud, penetrating voices, one of which was the well-known voice of the Captain. Our lamp had gone out and it was quite cold in the cabin. We heard the sound of oars outside, someone came on board and right over my head there was the clatter of a sabre. What was happening? we asked each other. We were only ten miles from that stretch where the rebellion was reported to be raging when we left Constantinople—perhaps it had now spread to the coast here.

People went down the stairway. Swords rattled on the steps. No one spoke. The first we saw was the Captain, with a lantern in his hand. He was followed by a heavily armed Tartar with a sheepskin cape over his shoulders and high cap; he was half-smothered with mud and his hair was dripping wet. He went over to Philippovich and a conversation began in Turkish; one could understand the half of it from the Tartar's gesticulation. He spoke of attack, fighting and death. Several times he grabbed one of his pistols or rattled his sword, rolling his eyes around in his head.

Only after he left us with the Captain did we get the whole story clear. The Tartar was one of the couriers carrying letters and dispatches from Widin to Constantinople; he knew that all his comrades had been seized and were being held prisoner in Nish and Sofia and he had therefore tried with his escort to avoid these places. But he did not succeed; his companions were shot and he himself had managed to reach this bank of the Danube where he knew that our Austrian steamer was due to pass that night. He had sat here in the reeds and waited. When we came he called out and now wanted to go with us up along the Serbian bank to Radejevacz, from where he would try to find another and happier route.

May 10, 1841

We all stood in the sunshine. We had passed Oreava; on both sides of the river the land was flat. It was unpleasant on deck. The Turks had spread out filthy carpets and blankets. My Frankish companions spoke of insect-emigration—the second class passengers confirmed this and the Captain nodded. One did not know where one dared to walk. In addition to this there was a great washing and cleaning of leeches going on. In Nicopolis we had taken four French leech-merchants on board; these men collected their living wares in Bulgaria; millions of leeches make the journey to France each year. They have to be washed and looked after and therefore, as I said above, a washing and scrubbing was going on. The wretched creatures were put into bags, hung up on strings so that the water could drip away. Some of them went for a walk on deck or climbed the rigging. One of the ship's boys had bleeding feet—a leech had fastened on and bitten hard.

We sailed past the Bulgarian town of Zibru. The horizon was bounded by the proud snow-decked Balkan mountains. A flock of storks walked about on the green fields where there was a cemetery, unenclosed, with white gravestones. Some fishing nets were spread out—it was a very pleasant landscape. But there was no calm on our vessel. The waves on the Danube were like those on a stormy lake; the ship bobbed up and down and the sea-sick chambermaid sat, very pale, leaning up against the Captain's cabin and whispered, "It is dreadful, it is just like being at sea." But it was not like being at sea—there was really only a little rocking!

The town of Lom-Palanka now appeared; it was quite considerable, with bush-covered hills and leafy scented gardens stretching down to the river. The Turks, true men of gold according to the Turkish proverb that "speech is silver, silence is golden," sat motionless as dolls and smoked their pipes; they did not once turn their heads to look at us.

The wind whistled in the rigging; the waves rose higher and higher as if they were dancing in a storm. I had never before thought of such a wave-dance on a river. The chambermaid was as sea-sick as she could be. Father Marco sang and assured the girl that it was weather for a baby's baptism; he even put up a sail which he called *una Phantasia*, because he said it looked nice, rather than being of any real use.

Widin, the strongest fortress of Bulgaria, lay before us with its five and twenty minarets. Cannons peered out of the emplacements. A throng of people stood by the landing stage. Turks reclined on their wooden balconies and drank their coffee. Soldiers were drawn up so that no one from our ship should come into the town and bring in plague contagion from the always-suspect Constantinople. There was much life and movement in the motley clad crowd. Finally we lay alongside the low bridge; a great ladder was set up and planks laid up from it to the ship. Now we were allowed to disembark. Close by there was a little wooden house in which there was a shovel of smoking embers. Each of us who wanted to go round the town had first to go into this house and be fumigated so that any infection in our clothes and bodies might be dispelled. It was very difficult to balance on those loose planks and the ladder was quite steep; the good-natured Turks gave us a helping hand down, then quickly left us and then we were smoked in order not to infect them. Everyone in Widin knew that Philippovich was on board and that he was to have an audience with the Pascha; he therefore was not fumigated since this would have caused delay. A beautiful horse was waiting for him, already saddled; he mounted and rode off to Hussein Pascha's palace, to talk about the measures to be taken regarding the couriers who had been taken prisoner and also about the onward passage of the letters and dispatches. Pascha of the Three Horses' Tails refers to the standard of the Bey or Emir: a horse's tail suspended from a pole and surmounted by a golden ball. Viziers had a right to three tails, and Grand Viziers to five. Hussein is Pascha of three horses-tails and is well known for his energy and fight against the Janissaries in 1826, which ended with the abolition of the whole band. In 1828 he opposed Diebitsch at Schumla for a long time, but was less fortunate in 1832 against Ibrahim Pascha in Syria—after which he became Pascha in Widin.

We stepped on land and were fumigated; all the goods on the other hand—even sacks of wool—were exempted. Then we walked about the town which, after heavy rains, was dreadfully dirty. The streets near to the harbor were like a morass; in some places we saw a sentry sitting on a muddy stone—I say sitting, but in fact he was squatting on his haunches, his bare knees sticking through holes in his trousers. He held his knife in a half-resting position that looked rather comical. In Widin we all visited, for the last time, a kind of Turkish craftsman whose skill reaches its height in this country—the barber. The barbers are quite remarkable here. Admittedly they lather, so near as not to matter, the whole of your face and play with your head as though it were that of a puppet; but they have such dexterity and lightness that you think that a feather is gliding over your face, when in fact it is a sharp knife. The face is shaved three times and then perfumed all over. To this can be added that one need not now, as was the case some years ago, be afraid that they would shave one's hair off! Now they know that the Franks like to keep their hair and so they have even begun to let their own grow.

That evening Hussein Pascha sent us a bundle of the most recent German newspapers—Hussein takes the *Allgemeine Zeitung* and now indeed we got to know what was happening in the country we had bypassed.[1] It was really food for the soul to get these papers, the best nourishment that Hussein could have sent us.

We made ourselves very comfortable. The ship lay still and peaceful; it was dead calm, rather sultry. We looked forward to a good night's sleep.

But then came unrest again! We were awakened by a flash, as though everything were in flames and the noise was as if the fortress had fired off its 280 cannon. It was a Bulgarian thunderstorm and old Zeus, or Thor—whichever of them still rules up in the clouds—was roaring away over us. One clap of thunder followed another without pause; wave upon wave roared in our ears, just as the waves of the Danube

---

[1] We also found this paper in Athens and Constantinople; my companions had found it in Jerusalem and Babylon. It is indeed a paper that has become *allgemein*. HCA.

broke before our eyes. Every second the whole landscape was lit up in the day-clear lightning. We were all awake on deck; only the Turks slept sound, swathed in their woolen cloaks, their faces covered.

We had left Widin and lay near the little township of Florentin. Wretched mud-huts lay close to the river bank; the ruins of a Turkish bath-house stretched out into the Danube and here we saw the first cliffs. We saw velvet-green meadows with groups of horned cattle and shy horses. This was not a picture to be seen by daylight; it was a picture painted by the lightning—the white minaret, the waving poplars, the fleeing horses, the surging river—words cannot describe what seemed to me to be a flight from reality. . . .

Through the Iron Gate

A little river which flows into the Danube forms the boundary between Bulgaria and Serbia. The whole country seems to be one enormous oak forest and the green tree is sacred: whosoever cuts down a tree, they say, takes a life. . . .

The different characteristics of people and cultures appeared at once here in the various guard-houses on the border, which lie so close to each other that the soldiers in one could shout over to those in the next house.

On the flat grassy plains of Wallachia, with its clayey slopes going down to the river, lay a wretched mud hut, without windows. It had a chimney and a thatched roof of reeds. There was a group of men in long skin smocks. On the Bulgarian side, where the nature of the country was about the same as in Wallachia, there was a house of black stone. A fat Turk in a jacket, looking like a pug-dog on its back legs, was the border guard. In Serbia on the other hand there were wooded, tree-grown mountains. The guard-house was a friendly white building with a red roof. Everything was smiling, lively and green. The soldier appeared to be half warrior, half shepherd.

"Goodbye, land of the Bulgars!" we shouted, and glided on beneath the woods of Serbia.

The first town here, small though it was, with its red roofs and clean appearance, transported us straight into the middle of Germany. Nine storks were taking their promenade in the fields. The sun-spirit of Africa had perhaps newly brought summer into the town with them. The temperature was 30 degrees C.

The Serbian loves his trees, as the Swiss loves his mountains, and as the Dane loves the sea. Under the crowns of the trees the city

representatives are assembled each year with Prince Milosh;[1] the trees
are arched into a court of law; under the trees the bride and bridegroom
dance. The tree stands like a very warrior and fights against the enemies
of Serbia. . . .

At Radejewacz the Tartar Hasan left us, with all our best wishes—
that he might reach Constantinople safe and sound. At this point the
island of Ostrava begins. On the Wallachian side there were the first
considerable woods we had seen and cultivated vineyards. It was as
though the forest richness and culture of Serbia threw a luster not
only over the Danube island but over the Wallachian side too. The
birds sang as I have heard them sing in the Danish beech woods. We
sailed through a small arm of the Danube as if we were gliding through
a lovely wood. The sunlight quivered through the green branches and
shimmered on the moving water. A young Serbian girl, with red
ribbons on her white jacket and shining coins around her red cap,
stood by the stream with her water pitcher—it was a living illustration
to the Serbian song:—"The maiden went to get water, she leaned
towards it and quietly said these words to herself. 'Poor child, how
beautiful you are! With a garland you would look much more beautiful,
you would dare to love the shepherd, the young shepherd who goes
before his flock, like the moon before the army of stars!' "

Among warlike people, where the woman is not an Amazon but
just a woman, she has to be silent and humble herself. The subordinate
position of the Serbian women does not allow them to express their
deepest feelings—but these are revealed characteristically in all their
love-songs.

During the last year, Prince Milosh has had a rich treasure collected
of the many songs of this country, many celebrating the heroic deeds
of the whole people.

In a Serbian house several couples often live together, but they
choose one as the chief who manages the money and household affairs;
in the evening there is the sound of cheerful music, of violin and
bagpipe. In every house there is always one person who can play and

---

[1] Milosh played a leading role in the uprising against the Turks in 1804. He established himself
as ruler of Serbia, was elected Prince in 1817, and was a founder of the Obrenovitch dynasty.

with his instrument lead the heroic songs. In this way the children learn their history; in this way the love of country is maintained and strengthened in the old.

The evening was still and mild. The Danube flows here in the same latitude as the Arno; the stars twinkled and the Serbian woods stood high against the translucent air. The night was so clear that we were able to continue sailing all the time and we had put considerable distance behind us when I came up on deck the next morning, just as we were passing the Turkish fortress of Fetislam on the Serbian side. The roof of the great tower was quite in decay; only the laths were in place. It was gloomy sight. Some of its company sat in the wall emplacements, smoked tobacco and stared after us. At 8 o'clock we were at Kladovo. Passengers and goods were transported in a large, beautifully painted boat with a wooden awning. The so-called *Iron Gate* begins here, which most travel-writers describe as that part of the Danube which is almost impossible to navigate. Here there are powerful falls and mighty whirlpools which have swallowed up boats and torn ships apart; round about in the foaming stream black rocks stretch their crushing fingers up into the air. But yet one can sail through the Iron Gate, and I found the later trip between Orsova and Drencova far more wild and dangerous.

Our excellent Captain stationed himself forward in the boat, which was dragged up against the current by fifty or so Serbs on land, hauling a rope with an iron chain. Under the bank lay a mass of river boats; the gang of Serbs had to jump from ship to ship like mountain goats, haul and haul, then jump into their fragile boats and with the rope around their waists row themselves and us forward.

We kept ourselves close into the Serbian bank; in midstream were some falls, and the water spurted up against the prow of the ship. In a couple of places the bank rose up in low but vertical cliffs. In these, like a kind of railing, ropes were fixed, by which our Serbs in their small boats held themselves fast and so worked against the stream. Then they sprang on land again and our little vessel went like a steam engine against the powerful river. It did not look at all dangerous, but it was very peculiar. Old trees hung out from the mountains, the nightingales sang and our big flag with the double eagle fluttered in the wind. A little beyond the small town the most dangerous part of the journey through the *Iron Gate* begins. All the passengers went ashore and only the Captain and the sailors stayed on board. It was not danger that drove us off but green wood that invited us—it was fresh, scented and very pleasant. The Serbian border-soldiers who had followed us from Kladovo took care that we should not come into any sort of contact with the people of the country.

To walk on land after several days of walking up and down on the ship's deck—with the exception of the short visit in Widin—this alone was refreshing, and it was doubly so here, in the middle of a scented wood and on soft grass covered with flowers. We each picked a bunch. Behind the trees high cliffs covered by bushes rose up, the green was spattered with the golden yellow of laburnum. We came upon a very large tree and were told that the former Pascha of Orsova had daily taken his luncheon here and that, not infrequently, just on these very branches, he had hanged some Christians. Not far from here was a Cross—it was the first Cross I had seen since I left Italy and it greeted me like a dear, holy sign from the land of the Crescent. Those green trees, these flowers and the song of the birds—it was a feast day in Nature. Our guard had enough to do to keep the company together— one wanted to pick a branch of laburnum, another to pick flowers, a third to drink spring water, and we dared not get parted from each other; we had to keep pace with the boat which, right enough, was making slower progress here, rocking a little and now and then getting well sprayed when cutting through the waves. The herdsmen and women whom we met fled, and looked at us from a respectful distance.

We passed a sulphur spring; a poor path led up to it—perhaps in not so many years there will be splendid baths here, with guests walking under these leafy trees. Our excellent skipper sat at the helm; the boat rocked like a leaf in the surf and the old man nodded to us as the water spurted up in the air. . . .

The Pascha in Orsova

We lay off the Turkish fortress of Orsova: it was the seat of a Pascha. The most dangerous part of the *Iron Gate* was passed and we were getting near to the first goal of our journey—quarantine. We went on board again, luncheon was ready and a farewell toast was drunk to the Crescent.

The Wallachian coast, with its tree-covered mountains, looked just like the Serbian side. On the right, on a projecting tongue of land, lies New Orsova with red-painted houses, white minarets and leafy gardens. We were told that the biggest building, out towards the river, was the Pascha's seraglio. Behind the well-latticed windows lovely women were looking at our boat. Perhaps they trained a spy-glass on us; they surely had one in order to see what kind of foreigners were now arriving soon to be locked up in quarantine—locked up as they were, but without the happiness of love. Below them they could see the fortress, which rises up from the Danube on the Serbian side; they could see their lord and master, the Pascha of Orsova, walking with his soldiers outside the walls, down to our boat which now lay still.

The Pascha, a powerful man of about 40 years, wearing a fez and a blue military great-coat with big gold epaulettes, greeted us and had a long conversation with Philippovich.

The fortress, which looks rather tumble-down, saluted us with five rounds of cannon as we glided past. We could now see the Austrian city of Old Orsova and the settlement of Zupaneck where the quarantine station was. We had to pass Orsova completely because of the strong current; only farther upstream was it possible to make the crossing.

The landing stage was enclosed with wooden railings, which creaked as the throng of sightseers leaned against them to look at the plaguey foreigners!

163

Large wagons, yoked with oxen, took up our baggage and moved off; the company followed slowly, escorted by soldiers and quarantine officers, each with a long white stick to keep us three steps away from himself.

The fortress lay in shadow, but in New Orsova the minarets, roofs and trees shone in the most beautiful sunshine. A boat set out across the river towards the Pascha's seraglio—it was the Pascha himself, going to visit his wives. We were going to our locked prison, he to his flowering terraces, kisses and embraces. The lot of each man is different in this world—that is the moral of this story.

Quarantine

May 12–22, 1841

To be in quarantine is to give one practice in the art of being a polyp! In fact, of course, all of us in this world are in quarantine, until we are allowed to make the great journey to heaven. I have known travelers who lie abed until noon and before they are up and dressed it is afternoon, and then they have to write letters or an account of what they did the previous day, before they have time to go out and see a gallery. In this way they take a year to see what others see better in a month; but this is called being solid, not being careless and superficial. I call such people quarantine-folk. I have a completely opposite character: on a journey I must rush about from morning till evening; I must see and see and see. There is no time to do anything but to pack cities, people, mountains and oceans into one's mind— always taking in, always remembering. There is no time to sing a single song—indeed I am not really in the mood for it—but it will come, that I know. Inside it bubbles away and ferments and when I am in the good city of Copenhagen and am given both a spiritual and literal cold shower, then the flowers shoot out! The treatment is not the best one might wish, but who asks me what I want? In the end I really believe that it does me good. . . .

Our entry into quarantine was a subject for a painter. All around were wooded mountains with a flat green slope in front. Here the artist could begin by picturing the heavy wagons filled with our baggage—wagons drawn by white oxen and driven by Wallachian peasants in coarse white smocks with colossal hats hanging down over their shoulders; and then he could add the motley company of Turks, Greeks and Franks. Pater Adam in his black gown, with a hat like a great shield was not the least picturesque figure. Soldiers followed as escort. The entry was very cheerful! We saw cannon, bare walls, great padlocks, keys that rattled and quarantine officers who drew themselves respectfully to the side in order not to come into contact with us. The "highway," the so-called promenade in between the high walls, was so bare that it almost had the attraction of novelty. True enough, there were a couple of rose bushes, but the roses themselves lay in quarantine in the green bud; every leaf reminded us of our quarantine flag. I will not complain about the accommodation, but only describe it; I will not bewail the food—even though sauerkraut and Danube water with pork is not to my taste.

The whole building is like a box within a box. The central part is a kind of square garden, the core of which is a little arbor of unpainted, raw laths up which the plants did not seem to have the courage or strength to climb. Four wings, in which every window is double-barred, enclose this Paradise—which one dared to look at but not to touch. Outside, around the wings, there is yet another great wall; each tiny cell inside has a little courtyard. The wall has yet another wall around it—and the space between is the promenade. It is pleasanter to read about this than to experience it in reality! The Englishman, Ainsworth, and I shared two small rooms, each furnished with nothing more than a table, a chair and a truckle bed. For the rest, the walls had been newly white-washed and were fairly clean. The blessed sun shone through and on to the walls so that one was almost blinded with its glory. As our keeper we had an old fellow called Johan who had been at the Battle of Leipzig and had there got a scratch—he had to have some memento of the fact that he had actually been in battle! He slept each night on the dining table in our hall.

The first day in quarantine goes excellently; one rests after the journey. The second, third and fourth days one writes letters, the fifth and sixth one has got into the routine and reads a good book—if he has one. But on the seventh day one steps out of routine again and discovers that the seventh day should be a day of rest, but not that the whole seven days should be so. I began to despair, even though we had daily visits from the swallows, who had built their nests in our ante-room and flew around the place telling us the *Chronique Scandaleuse* from the good city of Orsova. In our courtyard there were two scented lime trees—I often flung my arms around them and then,

Quarantine. Andersen drew the quarters where he spent his Danube quarantine walking in the box-like courtyard with its bare walls. PHOTO COLLECTION GRACE THORNTON

in the end, sat on a branch—and then up on to the next one. From there I could see over the wall, to a whole bit of mountain with woods and arable land and right between them a little hut—it looked just like paradise because there one was free! From my green awning I could see down into a row of neighboring yards. Philippovich had planted a Turkish horse's tail in front of his door, the brass button gleamed in the sun, the long white and red horse-hair hung round the colored stock. The leech dealers washed and rinsed their black leeches, which they kept in bags and sacks. Bulgarian women surrounded by children lay in groups on their blankets and held large yellow umbrellas over themselves against the sun. They were surely telling stories, for the children chortled and the swallows flew around and twittered offensively, for the swallows here were only concerned with every-day stories of things just seen from the nest.

During the first days in quarantine we had music, and good music too. Two young Wallachian artists, a flutist, a glass-harmonica player, gave concerts in their little prison cell; their music sounded over the whole garden. Their fellow prisoners peered out from all the windows and at the end applauded—because it was artistically very good. The flutist breathed feeling and taste—the music refreshed us. One evening he played so cheerfully the hymn "Rejoice in life!" but in here it sounded like an insult. It was all right for him—he was going out the next day, but we had to hold out for another seven days.

But it was also possible to take walks around the building between the high white walls; one could peer through the trellis into each little court, read on the little blackboards written in chalk, the day and time the foreigners had been incarcerated, the day and time they would be let out, and how many there were inside. It was reading matter for fantasy and the heart—who was the stranger, where did he come from or was it perhaps a she? Here was an opportunity to share common suffering. But, on this promenade, one dare not give way completely to imagination and emotion—it was necessary to stick closely to one's keeper and discretion, so as not to risk any extension of the quarantine period. Sometimes one met later arrivals and then one had to keep close to the wall in order not to touch them. The wind must not carry so much as a little feather over the wall, for it might alight on our shoulders; one must be careful not to touch a thread that someone had dropped—because that would extend the quarantine.

I used to take this walk simply to ensure that my feet should not forget how to move. No one walked here for enjoyment; one was more than anxious—one was almost terrified at meeting a load of goods, for just to come into contact of any sort would mean the beginning of a new 40-day quarantine. It was so warm between these walls and inside our little court that we were almost boiled. During the day I dreamed that I was in the lead chambers of Venice and at night that I was wide awake and living in Hell.[1] In the end we were

---

[1] I had learned recently from letters that, in his new satire, Heiberg had told of the performance in Hell of two of my large-scale dramatic works. I had not given this a thought so long as I was in God's free air, but here, as I said, in this Hell I dreamed that I was imprisoned in a Heibergian inferno and sure enough it was just as he had recounted—only my pieces were performed and

all sick and the doctor prescribed a remedy which seemed to me first-class for Wallachian horses, but not for weak human beings with upset stomachs: first one should drink a large glass of aquavit and then a cup of strong coffee, without sugar or cream.

Even the least varied life has its big moments and ours in here had three. The first was a visit from the Pascha of Orsova. The bare arbor in the garden served as the reception room. Six soldiers with bandoleers over their blue jackets and fixed bayonets made up the escort, with an interpreter, doctor and servants. The second great event was that we were each given an old washerwoman to wash our clothes, and therefore to see out the quarantine with us. We got our keeper's wife. The old couple slept in the corridor on the dining-table; a rolled up jacket served as pillow and a military coat as blanket—everything as in camp! The third event began with music and declamation. Through the window of a room across the garden came the sound of frightful shouting and crying from some of the fellows locked up there. Seven years ago they had fled from Austria over into Wallachia, had lived there, but were now very homesick and were going back of their own free will. They had given themselves up and now, before they were handed over, had to undergo quarantine. Before the sun rose and far on into the dark evening, they talked or played on Bulgarian flutes, but always the same piece of two or at the most three notes. It sounded as if one was whistling through a tulip leaf and at the same time treading on a cat's tail!

At last the hour of our liberation struck, but the guards had a dinner party or whatever it was—a whole hour longer than our sentence, a whole hour that seemed like a whole day to wait. And then this did not happen cheerfully as when we had arrived, for we were weak and we who had so much looked forward to freedom, had lost the use of

---

this pleased me very much; yes, as a Christian soul it was particularly pleasing to learn that, as he also told us, after seeing my plays the damned could rest with a good conscience. Even down there I had achieved some good with my work. Incidentally, I also heard down there that it had one evening been decided that in addition to my two plays Heiberg's *Fata Morgana* would be given as the concluding piece—but the damned had protested; even Hell can be made too hot and there must be moderation in all things! The devil could let it be enough with my two pieces, but he was determined that they should be succeeded by the newest all-hell's comedy that Heiberg has given us. . . . That is the sort of dream one has in quarantine! HCA.

The Visit of the Pascha of Orsova to the Quarantine Camp. Andersen made this drawing on the 15th of May, 1841 when the Pascha, accompanied by six soldiers, an interpreter, doctor and servants, made a visit to the camp and were received in the bare arbor in the garden. PHOTO COLLECTION GRACE THORNTON

our wings—we were out of practice. As the passenger from a ship often still has the feeling of sea-sickness—and we all still had the feeling of quarantine. For a long time afterwards poetic memory-pictures were reflected in my thoughts, and these showed me the poor little house up between the fields and the wood that I had spied from the tree. They let me hear the sound of the flute, of the young artist from

Bucharest; they let me experience again the Sunday service in our prison when Ainsworth sat quietly and read his Bible, Pater Adam sang mass with his Armenian boys and I looked at the green vineleaves by my lattice, where God's sun shone so warm that my thoughts flew out into Nature—where one is always with the heart of God.

Journey from Orsova to Drencova

May 22–25, 1811

The greater part of the Danube passage between Orsova and Drencova is far more dangerous to sail than through the *Iron Gate*. The currents are stronger and swifter, the falls are bigger and more frequent, the whirlpools are far more extensive. It was on this trip a couple of years ago that the boat carrying steamship passengers capsized and all met their death in the river. It was, they said, a gray rainy day, there was a fair amount of wind, the Captain stood at the tiller, the boat was full of travelers. It was no easy maneuver to steer between the rocks jutting out all around in the river. A crowd of peasants on land dragged the boat through the strong eddies, while the storm flung the spray high into the air. The Captain shouted to the gang to pull more slowly, but they did not hear him—the storm and stream drowned his cries. He repeated his command yet again—they misunderstood him and hauled even faster and that moment the boat hit a rock, turned over and no rescue was possible. Far from the spot where the accident took place, some of the bodies were found—among others a young Englishman, whose family have raised a memorial close by the river where his body was found and where he was buried.

Since this accident happened the steamship company has not allowed their passengers to make this part of the journey by boat; they must ride or be driven. An excellent highway is being constructed and is nearly finished. In some places the rocks have been mined and where the ground was loose and marshy the stone has been used to strengthen and fill it in. All the cargo is taken by boat, drawn by horses, the day before the foreigners leave.[1]

---

[1] The iron steamship *Stephan* which goes between Vienna and Linz, had, 14 days before I came this way, tried to go with the stream right down to Orsova—and it was a success. On the other hand the journey back had been slow, in spite of the power of the engine and by *Ishla* they had had to harness 14 horses to draw them, because here the current and eddies were stronger than

Early in the morning of May 24; the wagon was waiting outside the hotel and we rolled away. It was the most beautiful summer weather; everything looked green and fertile. I have never seen so many butterflies as on that morning; they were all white and all the trees were so covered with them that one thought one was seeing flowering fruit trees. The postillion cracked his whip on all sides and the butterflies flew up into the air, like snowflakes in winter.

Here, on this stretch of the military border, live Wallachian peasants. We drove through a couple of their very picturesque villages. There were great cracks in the clay walls, and paper pasted over the holes which should serve as windows. A kind of door, tied with strips of bark to some laths, formed the entrance to a yard which was usually swarming with herds of pigs and an incredible number of children, as good as naked, tumbling over each other; even girls of 9 or 10 years were totally naked. Round about were lovely trees, in particular chestnuts, large and sweet-smelling. Individual peasants we met stood upright in their carts and jogged away like the ancient Romans on the race-course.

The countryside became more and more romantic—it surpasses the Rhine in its beauty. By Plavisovicza, where the Kazan Narrows are found, the Danube runs between vertical cliffs; the road has been cut into the mountain, the rock masses hang over the traveler's head like a smoothed ceiling. For a long stretch there is one large cave after another—one of them is so deep that, I was told, it takes an hour and a half to go through it and then one comes out into a valley on the other side of the mountain. The best known here is the so-called *Veterani-Cave*. We stopped outside it, but could not see the entrance. The whole mountain is grown over with bushes and climbing plants and between the hedges runs a little path. It was very steep and there were a lot of loose stones, but we had the green branches to hang on to and we easily came up a few yards over the roadway to an entrance, comfortably big enough for any well-grown man. For a couple of steps

---

the engine horse-power. A new and bigger steamer, I do not remember of what power, is now under construction and the Danube Company hopes that this will be able to sail up against the current on this, the most violent stretch of Europe's longest and most powerful river. HCA.

inside one had to stoop a little, but soon the rock face widened out again to a fairly considerable, if gloomy, chamber. From this one came into an enormous hole where the light streamed down through a large opening, of which the topmost rim was overgrown with bushes and long trailing climbing plants, which formed a flowering frame for the blue sky.

The cavern consists of an endless number of sections; we went over to one of the nearest—I was in the front and stopped at the most surprising sight. In the middle of the floor a large fire had been lit, a pot was boiling and all round lay and stood white-clad men and women, with mulatto-colored faces and long black hair. Quick as cats, two youths sprang towards me, stretched out their hands in entreaty and addressed me in a language I did not understand. It was a whole gypsy family. Two old ones sat by the fire; their hair hung down thick and coarse around their ugly faces—the way they were sitting meant that I did not know for certain whether they were two men or two women. Our company gave each of the young men a small tip; one of the children got a silver coin from me—at once one of the older girls sprang up, grabbed my hand, dragged me to the fire, looked into my palm, bowed three times down to the ground and told my fortune. But I understood not one word of it. The translation of the prophecy which a young man from Bucharest gave me later—or what he had been able to make out of it seemed to have been more appropriate to a rich Englishman than to a Danish poet. "Your silver shall turn to gold," she had said, "and your estate grow from year to year." To my question as to whether the girl had foretold anything bad for me, he told me that she had said I would have least joy from my daughters! And in this she had hit on the truth, as far as the writer is concerned— for *Agnete* and *Maurerpigen*[2] have brought me but little happiness—I must clearly see about getting myself sons! The rest of the company also had their fortunes told, but apparently I was the most fortunate of the lot.

Late in the day we reached the village of Tissowiza (now Tishovitsa)

---

[2] *Agnete* and *The Moorish Girl* were two of Andersen's less successful plays. In fact, the financial and critical disaster of *The Moorish Girl* helped decide Andersen to make this trip.

where we were to enjoy a meal in a poor inn. The host had not been warned that the steamship passengers were due that day and when he was totally unprepared we came upon him. He had quickly to go and chase up all the village chickens. The lower story of the house consisted of two stone cellars; above these there was a very rickety wooden balcony going the length of the house, from which one entered a hall where there was a chimney and where the food was prepared. On each side was a gloomy and dirty room; we all preferred the open air and therefore camped out under the tall shady chestnuts. Most of us were still sick from quarantine and I felt particularly unwell.

After a couple of hours' stop our wagon rolled on its way again, still along the Danube. We passed the remains of three great towers from Roman times, built close up to the river and now used as guard posts. A wooden bridge led out to them from the road. Armed border soldiers sat and played cards or leaned against the wooden railings. Almost the whole road here is an avenue of lovely walnut trees; as we passed in our haste, we broke off some scented leaves and with a branch as fan protected ourselves against the burning sun, when there was no shade from the trees. It was terribly hot and we were fainting from thirst. The road that had been built came to an end and the pathway was so narrow that one wheel touched the cliff wall and the other was not more an inch or two from the bank above the swirling river. We drove along at a walking pace, but finally this looked too dangerous and we had to get out, but we could only do this by crawling down from the back of the wagon, since there was no foothold on either side.

A new hazard then occurred which could have had unpleasant consequences. The road on the Serbian side, which was cut through the rocks in the time of Trajan is in our day not fit for use. Under military escort the Serbs therefore have to haul their boats along the military border. The consequence of coming into the slightest contact with these people, or with the long rope with which they haul the ship, would have been anathema. We saw now in front of us about a hundred Serbian peasants all screaming who were dragging a very large ship upriver. It was very slow work against the strong currents;

we had to drive at a snail's pace because nowhere was the road broad enough for us to pass. All the pangs of quarantine were still in our blood. At that moment I could think of no more dreadful order than this—"Turn round again—into Quarantine!" Step by step, we drove, stopped, then went on again pace by pace, only to stop again. I had a feeling that I was going round the world with leaden weights around my legs.

At last there was a place where the road was a little broader than before and where the soldiers escorting the Serbs thought that we might be able to slip past. The tails of our horses were tied up so that they should not wave about and touch the rope; our luggage, even the leather curtains on the wagons, we drew in as close to ourselves as we could. The wretched Serbian peasants stationed themselves as far out on the river bank as they could—and all the same we were not more than about half a yard from them. And so we drove carefully and slowly past the whole long row of a hundred or so people—and if the whiplash had so much as flicked the edge of a single coat, then we should have been forced to turn around again to quarantine in Orsova.

How lightly we breathed and how the coachman drove his horses when we were past! We galloped through the woods, over fords and past rippling streams; green branches of the trees brushed against our faces and shoulders. Over copse and river the landscape opened out towards the little town of Drencova, where the steamship *Galathea* was waiting for us.

Before the year 1836 Drencova was only a guard-post; with the Danube steamship traffic it will soon be a small town. There were a number of quite considerable buildings, one of them an inn. About a day's journey from here the famous "Schiller" wine is made. I drank a toast in it for its namesake; the wine of the soul and spirit that he has given us can well be sent out to the countries of the world and it can only charm, not intoxicate.

We were very happy to board the spacious, beautiful steamer that was to take us to the capital of Hungary, and we looked forward to the many comforts it offered. "But no one knows his fate"—and with that saying we can end our day's journey.

In Pest a very large fair is held four times a year; people flock to the city from the farthest corners of the land and at these times especially, use is made of the steamships, which are overcrowded. Of course we were due in Pest two days before the great *St. Medardus Fair*. The inn-keeper warned us that it would be a very difficult journey, but we did not believe him and thought that he was trying to keep us there to look at the flowers until the next steamer arrived and in the meantime, to drink with him each evening a *skaal* to Schiller in Schiller!

As the sun went down, I walked alone into the woods close by and met some gypsies, who had lit a fire and were sitting around it. When I came out of the woods again a handsome young peasant boy was standing among the bushes; he greeted me with a good evening in German. I asked him if it were his mother tongue; he said no, that he usually spoke Wallachian, but had learned German in school. From his clothes he seemed to be very poor, but everything he had on was very clean, his hair was combed smooth, his eyes sparkled happily and there was something wise and good in his face, such as I have found in few other children. I asked him if he was going to be a soldier and he answered, "Yes, we all have to do that here, but I can also become an officer, so I am learning everything I possibly can." I told him that he must be an officer and that he certainly would achieve this, if he worked hard and trusted in the good God. To my question as to whether he knew Denmark, he thought a little and then replied, "I think it is a long way from here—near to Hamburg."

I could not give him money—he seemed too noble for that—so I asked him to pick me some flowers and he ran off and soon brought me a beautiful bunch. I took it and said, "I shall buy these flowers," and so he got his payment. He went quite red in the face and thanked me politely.

He told me his name was Adam Marco. I took a card from my pocket, gave it to him and said, "When you become an officer and perhaps come to Denmark, then ask for me and I shall be happy to share your good fortune. Be industrious and trust in God—and who knows what may happen!" I pressed his hand and he stood for a long time, looking at the ship as I went on board. . . .

From Drencova to Semlin

May 25 and 26, 1841

It was morning and for some time now we had been going at full speed. We had lost sight of Drencova; wooded hills rose on both sides of the river and a range of clouds hung like a suspension bridge between them. We sailed right under and it changed suddenly to a balloon-shaped cloud as the smoke from our boat mingled up with it. The country here was very picturesque. In the middle of the Danube there is a rock, shaped like a rhinoceros horn; it is called *Babakaj*. The word can be Turkish, Serbian and Slav—in Serbian it means, "Be quiet, old one!"; in Turkish "Father of the rocks" and in Slav, "Repent, old one!" This last explanation agrees with the legend that is attached to this rock. A jealous husband is said to have put his wife out here in the middle of the rushing river. The rock is big enough for someone to stand on quite comfortably and, if he is in the mood for it, he can enjoy a very attractive view. For on the Serbian side, on a mountain rising straight up from the river and adjoining dark stretches of forest, there rises the mountain fortress of Gobulaza (now Golubac), parts of which are from Roman times.

Soon we were passing Moldava, famous for its copper mines, and then the settlement of Bazias, with its poor little monastery. At every place we took a couple of additional passengers. One of these from the last stop was an elderly-looking gentleman who appeared to be a signet-engraver: he had his trade-mark over his stomach; more than a dozen seals of all sizes hung from his watch chain. He was a living map of the Danube—I owe to him the three-fold explanation of the name *Babakaj*.

Our one and only passenger from a town called Opalanka was a Madame; the moment the ship laid by, a man sprang on board with her suitcase and Madame shouted, "No, no—I'm going overland!" and she ran like a desperate lamb after the wolf which had stolen her

young—her large, well-strapped case. She was on the deck when at
the moment the steam puffed out of the funnel. In her terror she
stood stock-still, holding her yellow ticket in her hand. The conductor
took it and off we sailed. "But I'd rather go overland!" said Madame.
It was the first time in her life that she had ventured on to a steam
ship; she had been persuaded, talked round, and it was not her idea.
She assured us that she had not slept a wink the night before, thinking
about this trip. She was going a very long way, up to the city of
Vukovar—a whole two days' sailing! For the moment she had taken
a ticket only as far as Semlin, just to try it and to see that she was
not blown up. She was thrifty—she would not pay the whole journey
all at once, no, she would first see if she survived the first half! She
had heard of so many dreadful accidents with steam ships and steam
trains. "They are dreadful inventions," she said, "if only we are not
killed. . . . " and she looked anxiously all around. "The Captain
should keep closer in to the coast," she decided, so that one could
get ashore when the ship blew up. Our solid man with the seals gave
her a simple lecture about funnels, but she shook her head and understood not one word of it. I tried to translate it for her in yet more
popular, simpler terms and she appeared to understand me, for to every
sentence she said "Yes!" "Just imagine, Madame," I said, "that you
have a pot on the fire, which is cooking fast—there is a large lid on
it and if this is screwed down tight then the pot can blow up from
the hot steam inside. But if the lid is light and loose then it can bob
up and down, the steam can get out and the pot does not break."
"But, God help us," said Madame, "when the lid"—and she pointed
at the deck—"when the lid here over the steam engine bobs up and
down then we'll all fall into the Danube!" And now, clearly very
anxious, she held fast on to the railings.

Towards midday we passed Kubin over which there was a majestic
thunder-storm. The clouds formed a great dark Alp-land, with the
lightning as the mountain path, going zig-zag, up and across. The
thunder rolled, not like the sound of avalanches, but as though the
mountains themselves were falling. And it was very hot. The air was
oppressive and clinging. Wretched Madame was even hotter than we

were, since she had pulled her vast shawl over and around her so that she could neither see nor hear, and sat with beating heart waiting for the explosion that was bound to come! I advised her to go down to the ladies' saloon, but she answered no, with a wave of her hand. She could no longer talk.

This oppressive heat, this indolence, made one feel boredom and inertia; and indeed it looked as if the tumble-down fortress had itself collapsed for the same reasons. The Danube waters were quite yellow. On deck, folk sat and slept under their umbrellas. Everything we touched was burning hot. Madame had one glass of water after another. She took camphor drops on sugar. I am sure that she would have fainted had she only been certain that the ship would not choose that moment to explode. The next place we passed was Pancevo, a town in which it is said that it is the custom for young and old, even for the poor, to make up their faces. When the ladies weep over a romance it is possible to count their real tears: they appear as rose-red spots on the white pages of the book!

The sun went down but the heat was still sweltering. The new moon lit up, right over the fortress of Belgrade. On the German side there was heavy lightning. Lights moved here and there on the coast; we shot past the rushing Sava River. It was quite dark. A few minutes later we lay still, up by the bank outside Semlin (now Zemun), the first Austrian town on our right side. The Sava forms the border here with Serbia; from here we would leave the military frontier and cut through Hungary itself. All the steamships stay at Semlin for two nights and a day, so there was plenty of time for us to say goodbye to the last city with minarets. In the meantime Madame would not spend the night on the steamer; she had a relative in Semlin and would go and stay with him; yes—she would go quite away, this was her chance to go ashore.

It was morning. Everything was bathed in sunshine. The countryside was flat. To the left was a field with guard-houses built on stilts so that the guards should not be washed away whenever the Danube rose. To the right was Semlin, an ordinary market town. To the east was the fortress of Belgrade with its white minarets—which are the most characteristic feature in the physiognomy of the Orient. The fortress with its mosque lies on the top of a low mountain slope; outside it is the town which stretches down to the Danube and the Sava and is bounded on the other side by a vast oak forest. Belgrade has fourteen mosques; the right section of the city consists of the Turkish quarter, the center and the left is the Serbian quarter.

It was on the 25th of February, 1839, that the Serbs got their free constitution; the Turks now have only the fortress with the Pascha as Commandant. It was in the palace garden that the noble Greek, the poet Rhigas, was brutally executed. Greece was still Turkish. Rhigas was handed over to the Turks who, here in the court of the Pascha's palace, had him sawed in half—still living. In 1815 630 Serbs were impaled in this same place, alive. They had all surrendered on the promise of mercy. One of these unfortunates died only seven days later. The Danube streamed with bodies, with Serbian corpses. The Turk could sing, mocking, the Serbian song: "It is pleasant to sit by the river and see your enemy's broken weapons float by!" Down where the Sava joins the Danube there lies a ruined tower, *Nebojsa*—"Be without fear." From the emplacements here the bodies of the executed were thrown into the Danube. In this tower, in the deepest dungeon, where the river water oozed in, sat the noble Prince Jeffram Obren- owitsch, brother of Prince Milosh, who in single combat with the Pascha forced him to release his prisoner. The memories which are connected with this place awakened thoughts about the troll who, as the story goes, fastened his strong legs around the neck of Prince Agib. At the sight of that gloomy, ruined tower, I thought I could feel the damp walls closing in around me, like the wood-troll's legs! What terrors there are connected with this place, which now lay before us in lovely sunshine, with fresh green trees, sunlit minarets, domes and red-roofed houses!

Through the dark oak forest, down to the river Sava, fled "Black George,"[1] Serbia's first liberator. This forest and this river were the

---

[1] Black George (Czerny Djorde) was the original name of George Petrovic, founder of the Karageorgevic dynasty. He led the Serb revolt against the Turks in 1806, but was defeated by them in 1813. He fled to Austria, and on his return was murdered by Miloch Obrenovitch.

setting for one of the tragic scenes of this flight which still lives, and will always live, in the songs of the people. Black George fled with his old father, the shepherd Petroni. They were within sight of the river and the Austrian border and the father was overcome with sorrow at leaving his native land. He bade his son to give himself up, so that they could die on their ancestral soil. George wavered between filial duty and the desire for freedom; he was about to give in when the shouts of the Bosnians and Turks echoed through the forest. The son wanted to carry his father on his shoulders and swim with him over the river, but the old man would not leave the land to which his whole life and memories were bound; he would rather be cut down by those savage bands. Then the son asked for his blessing and the old man gave it to him, bared his breast, and the son shot him through the heart, threw the body into the Sava and then swam across the river. The waves told me this story and the dark oak trees nodded gravely and said, "Yes, this is how it was!" From the ruined tower, out of the open holes through which the bodies of Serbs were thrown, birds flew screeching, birds of prey that circle round what was once a place of execution.

Between the Austrian town of Semlin and the river Sava, stretching just outside Belgrade, there is a field on which a kind of market is held weekly. Two railings, set close by each other, separate the buyers from the sellers. Along the long narrow paths the Austrian guards and quarantine officers pace up and down with their long staffs, watching to make sure that no contact takes place, and that the Turkish goods are put into quarantine and the money first washed in vinegar before being received on the Austrian side. There was much shouting and gesticulation among the various people trying to make themselves understood; the wares were spread out and turned around again and again. Pigs, horses—all sorts of animals—were driven out into the river and submerged, and were then considered free from infection. Whips cracked, horns sounded and every other animal, quite terrified, ran up among the Turks and had to be driven out for a second soaking.

Towards evening the leading citizens of the good city of Semlin came on board and, one could see, they greeted each other according to rank; some received a low bow—they were the most important; others got a gracious inclination of the head which was laughable to see. In the end I thought I was at home—people are the same the whole world over!

There was a thunderstorm over the plains of Hungary; rain poured down over the home-going citizens of Semlin, both over the Number One in rank and over Number Twenty—such a stupid cloud does not recognize a Person's Consequence, but washes both high and low alike! After rain came shine, and everything gleamed again in the setting sun, on the ripples of the Danube and Sava, on the minarets of Belgrade. Here in the night I heard the last call from the minaret. When I came on deck again the next morning I knew that there would be nothing more on the river banks to remind me of the Orient—I had seen the last minaret.

Visitors to the Fair

At each town new passengers came on board . . . From all sides people were streaming to the great Medardus Fair. Every sleeping place was taken, and we still had several days' journey to go . . . I was tired and sick of the Danube journey. That may not be very polite—but it is true! Our ship was absolutely crowded with people. We were three hundred persons, and more could be expected before we got to Pest. Chests, sacks, parcels and packages lay heaped up—reaching up as high as the paddle-coverings. Round the deck and under the deck people tried to find a place—if not to sit, at least to stand. The most comfortable was a Turkish Jew who had been with us from Semlin; without any bother he kept the place he had taken originally. Very cheerfully, acting the clown for the whole company, he sat on a mat, holding between his legs a large flagon of wine. Every other moment he drank a *skaal*, nodded and sang, crowed like a cock and sighed like a maiden. A *heiduk* (foot soldier) in red trousers and a vast white cape stood unmoving with his back to the Captain's cabin, from morning to night. Some old Jews read aloud from their bibles in Hebrew. On some heaps of goods a couple of families sat and ate their onions and bread, played some kind of card game or dozed. A young officer paid court to a girl while two other officers joked with the little Armenian boy, Antonio, and to the horror of Pater Adam told the lad that he was too good to be a monk! They showed him their swords, twirled their mustaches and put their colored caps on his head. The boy smiled and Pater Adam shook his head. There was a generally cheerful atmosphere, chattering, noise and bustle everywhere. "Mein parapleem, parapleem!" screamed a Jew, whose umbrella had disappeared. "Felix faustumque sit"[1] called out a black-suited man who met a colleague.

---

[1] Be happy and of good fortune!

The wretched lady who had been with us from Constantinople dissolved into tears over the crowds and, as she said, the dreadful people in the second cabin. Certainly, one had to laugh or cry over it. Everything down there was wrapped in tobacco smoke. People stood pressed together—but there were also many who sat—and not only on the benches—but also on the tables. They sat there all day in order to have somewhere to sit at night. Two young Moslem ladies stood in the middle of the throng, holding each other round the waist and sniffing a lemon.

In the first saloon there was not much more room, but it was at least free of tobacco smoke. The gentlemen sat quite unconcerned among the ladies and played *Macau*—a game of chance—for very high stakes. A merchant from Semlin in a green gown and black felt hat, which he never took off even when he slept, had gambled away his watch and money. Champagne corks popped and there was a smell of roast beef.

Towards evening it was even worse. People were sleeping on the tables and benches, yes, even under the tables and benches, even on the window sills. Some lay fully clothed, others made themselves comfortable, pretending that they were about to get into their own good beds at home. In the ladies' saloon it was just as crowded; a couple of the oldest took, as one might say, courage and a man's heart and sat themselves inside *our* door. Others sat on the stairs, one above the other. The whole deck was one great sisterly-bed and here folk had retired already with the sun; one could not take a step without treading on them. There was such a muttering and sighing and snoring— and this we had to endure for two nights! One completely forgot the poetry of Nature for everyday life. At last, we saw the Hungarian flag—in airy mist. Pest lay before us. Buda was hidden by the high St. Gerard's hill, on the top of whose tower a flag was hoisted to greet the steamship which was bringing visitors to the Fair.

Pest and Buda

It is a remarkable view—but how does one paint it—and the sunlight in which it appeared—in words? The buildings along the river in Pest looked like a series of palaces. What life and traffic there was! Hungarian dandies, merchants—both Jews and Greeks—soldiers and peasants all mingle together. It is the St. Medardus Fair. Under the high green hill on the opposite bank of the river is a line of smaller but colored houses, with two rows stretching up the hillside. This is Buda, the capital of Hungary; its fortress, the Hungarian Acropolis, lifts its white walls over the green gardens. A bridge of boats joins the towns. And what a throng and tumult there is! The bridge rocks as wagons cross over. Soldiers march, bayonets glitter in the sun; a procession of countryfolk is on a pilgrimage. Now they are in the middle of the bridge, the Cross shines and the sound of a hymn is wafted over to us. The river itself is half full with ships and small boats. There is the sound of music. A flock of boats is rowed up stream, and from each boat Hungarian flags are waved by the dozen. The river bank is crowded with people; what sort of procession is this? All the people in the boat are, as near as no matter, naked, but with a tri-colored cap. The music clangs, flags wave, oars splash! What *is* going on? I ask a young lady who is also looking at this performance and she tells me that it is the military swimming-school officers and cadets; they all take part in a race down stream to St. Gerhard's Hill, but it is impossible to swim back and so they row in boats with flags and music. It looks attractive but it is certainly extraordinary!

We go ashore and find a hotel. It is very handsome, but disgracefully expensive. At Fair time there is no fixed price. We wander about in Pest—it is like Vienna—at least part of Vienna with the same shops and the same well painted colored signs. One would like to stop and look at them. The one on a coffee shop has in gilded letters *Kave-*

Haz and underneath is a picture showing "The heavenly coffee-spring." Angels are sitting at a table drinking coffee: one of the prettiest angels is taking coffee from a spring where, dark brown, it gushes out among the flowers. In one of the streets here there is a *Stock am Eisen*, just as in Vienna—a last reminder of the primitive forest by the Danube. Every wandering apprentice drove his nail into the tree, so long as there was a free spot, and the tree became a tree of iron, a tree of nails. Hercules himself did not own such a club!

Buda has one theater, Pest two, the smaller of which is The National Theater, where they perform only plays in Hungarian. The actors are good, the production good and the house is, I was told, always well patronized. This building is also used as a concert hall and here I heard, in Hungarian translation, Mendelssohn-Bartholdy's oratorio *St. Paul*. The Imperial State Theater is large and handsome, but badly lit.

But before we sail again we will take a little trip on the other side of Buda, to the grave of Gül Baba and bring the Turkish holy man a greeting from the Orient, from old Istanbul. Who is that in there, lying stretched out, face-down, a white felt hat without brim over his brow? Did I not see him in the whirling dervishes? It is a Dervish—he walked here all the way on foot, over the mountains, through desert plains, here to this alien people, to the Christians' city. His pilgrimage is ended; as a memory of it he hangs on the wall a colored, painted wooden sword—and then he throws himself on his face and mumbles, "There is no God but God and Mohammed is his Prophet". . . .

The Danube from Pest to Vienna

The steamer *Maria Anna* sails in the early morning to Vienna. We go on board; the little boat is crowded with people. It goes briskly upstream past the bath-houses where every timber bends under the weight of half-naked soldiers. One is wrapped in a coat, others in shirts—but now we have gone by.

Along this part of the river there once stretched vast primeval forests. Now a town greets us with churches and promenades. It is Waizen. There is a legend that shortly before the battle of Mogyorod in 1074 the Dukes Geza and Ladislaus rode through the forest, talking about the organization of the army. Suddenly Ladislaus shouted, "Didn't you see anything? While we were talking, an angel came from heaven and held a crown over your head. Now I know that you will be victorious!" And Geza answered, "If God is for us and your vision is fulfilled, then I will build a church in this place!" The enemies fled; a church was built here and the town of Waizen arose. . . .

Stories and legends abound all along this part of the river. The landscape of the countryside is varied with woods and hills, with green fields and populous towns. We approach a ruin—once upon a time, in its heyday, one of Europe's most enchanted castles. There were floors of marble, the ceilings shone with gold and the walls were covered with pictures and rich tapestries. . . . but all has vanished, all has gone. . . .

We came to Gran where St. Stephen[1] was born and where he now rests in his coffin. Up on the rock in the middle of the ruined fortress a church is under construction. The town itself lies flat, down among

---

[1] St. Stephen (c. 975–1083) was the first king of Hungary. He was canonized in 1087. His birthplace, Gran, was called Strigonium when Marcus Aurelius wrote twelve books of his Meditations there in the 2nd century A.D.

View of Czechoslovakia. The last leg of Andersen's journey took him up the Danube from Pest to Vienna, where he saw Hungary on one side of the river and Czechoslovakia on the other. NEW YORK PUBLIC LIBRARY PICTURE COLLECTION

green trees from which a whole mass of butterflies fly out over the Danube.

The journey the next morning offered us only the sight of flat wooded country on both banks of the river, with here and there a windmill, here and there a village with a church. Now we lay off Pressburg. As we pulled into the bridge a waiter threw a pack of cards out into the Danube—heaven knows why. The cards went deep down as if they were seeking the river-bed, but they floated up again—one in particular—and it was the Queen of Hearts; she bowed deep three times and then sank. That was our reception at Pressburg. Close by where we went ashore there was a little mound surrounded by walled fencing—this is very important because it is *Krönungs Berg*, around which the happy people assemble at the coronation of the king. From all the ships on the river the tricolor flag waves, cannons thunder and the King of Hungary—in the same costume and with the same crown that Stephen the Holy bore—rides up this hill and with his sword pointing to all four corners of the earth, swears to defend and preserve his land. The church bells, the trumpets, people and cannon all shout their "Long Live" for the Lord's anointed.

We are standing in the square in front of the townhall; on the wall over the door there is a picture painted *al fresco*. It shows an old man in a black gown with a long beard; he is bending over an open book. What does this mean, what is the legend? It is a horrible story. This man was, once upon a time, one of the city's most powerful counselors. He was an alchemist and astrologer, feared and hated. He knew how to appropriate everything to himself—even the poor woman's little plot of land. And the wretched woman marched into the town hall where he was sitting with the city's rulers. She wailed and complained in her desperation and exhorted him to swear on oath that he had dealt with the matter according to law and conscience; and he took the Book, bowed over it, read the oath with a hollow voice, raised his hand and swore. A whirlwind rushed through the room and every-- one fell to the ground. When it was still again and they raised themselves up, the perjurer had vanished; the window was broken and outside, on the wall, indelible, living in every feature as we still see it, there was the picture of the counselor of Pressburg. The devil had blown him into the smooth wall, like a colored silhouette.

Our steamship was on its way again; we met another boat, the *Arpad* on its way from Vienna and, like ours, overloaded with passengers. Hats and handkerchiefs waved, we saw ourselves mirrored in each others' eyes, and then the picture vanished again; only one of the many figures remains in the memory: a lady in a nankeen coat with a green spring-parasol. She has come to rest in my heart—I hope she is a respectable woman!

The whole of the morning, long before we had got to Pressburg,[2] we saw a thick strong cloud of smoke on the horizon. It was indeed

---

[2] Pressburg, now called Bratislava, was the capital of Hungary from 1541 until 1784. Several kings were crowned in the cathedral there. Andersen got some of the architectural details of this and other places from a copy of the *Wundermappe der Donau* with drawings by Thomas Ender, which he found in the saloon of the steamer.

Types of costume seen along the Danube.

a fire—and half Theben was burnt out that day. We approached this place at sunset—one of the most picturesque of the whole journey. High up the hill lay a ruin, surely the most beautiful on the whole length of the Danube. The red evening sun shone on the damp mill-wheel which, as it went round, seemed to be hammered out of gold.

Everything around was green and scented. How beautiful it was! Hungary's Theben is a little spot which has fallen from heaven. And here in all this loveliness there was wailing and need—half the town lay in dust and ashes; thick smoke was still rising from the fire. The roof of the church has fallen in, the black-smoked walls licked by the red flames. Many mothers were still looking for their children; a woman stood by the riverbank, wringing her hands. A burnt horse dragged itself over the bridge.

We passed by—we were in Austria! Next morning we would see Vienna. The journey from Constantinople to Vienna was thus (leaving aside quarantine) 21 whole days, and very tiring. From Vienna downstream to Constantinople takes 11 days.

Thin woods lay before us, stretching out into the distance. In the early morning the air was very thick and hot; it did not shine as over the Mediterranean and the Bosphorus. I thought I was at home on an oppressively warm summer day. My journey was now at an end. A feeling of depression tugged my heart, a premonition of something really bad. In little Denmark every talent stands so close to the next one that there is much jostling and pushing, for everyone wants his place. As far as I am concerned, they can only see my faults. My path at home goes through a very stormy sea. I know that many heavy waves will yet break over my head before I reach harbor. But this I know, that my future cannot be worse than my present. . . .

Part Five
JOURNEY HOME

Viennese Silhouettes

June 4–23, 1841

The great squares and main streets of Vienna present a spectacle like that of a picture gallery. Every shop has its beautifully painted sign, either a portrait of a well-known person or an allegorical piece. In every square and every street, with the animated crowd and different groups, there are themes for paintings which could decorate a whole gallery. But since sketches of this kind are always shown in great numbers, we will—for a change—cut out a couple of silhouettes give no more than a shadow of the real likeness.

We are in the Volksgarten; ladies and gentlemen are strolling under the green, sweet-smelling trees in lively conversation. Waiters rush about, criss-crossing the paths, in order to bring a little ice to burning hearts. The sound of music ripples through the garden. In the center of the band stands a young man; his big brown eyes, his head, his arms, his whole body are never still, as though he were the heart of the music—which indeed he is. The whole of Europe hears the beat of this musical pulse and its own pulse beats the faster. The man's name is *Strauss*. . . .

We are in one of the suburbs, a small palace lies in the middle of an English park; here lives Prince Dietrichstein. We pass through a series of beautiful rooms and are met by the sound of a pianoforte. It is all very handsome—there is a lovely view out over the terraced garden. The music we hear was written by one of the Princes of the piano. But Liszt does not play like this! He and this performer are equally great and equally different. Liszt astonishes—but here, on the other hand, one is refreshed by a feeling of peace and grace. . . . Who is this master of the piano?—It is Sigismund Thalberg.[1]

We are in the center of Vienna. We go up broad, stone stairs

---

[1] Sigismund Thalberg (1812–1871) was a piano virtuoso and composer.

between thick cold walls. There are great iron doors with padlocks on both sides, behind which are stored money and valuable papers. We enter a small room. The walls are covered with bookcases in which there are great folios; bundles of manuscripts lie all around—all state affairs. A tall, serious man sits behind a desk—it is not poetic affairs which occupy him. The harsh expression in his face changes to sadness. He looks at us with a soulful, thoughtful expression. In his youth he sang for us of the conflict in his soul and gave us *Die Ahnfrau*; in his maturity he brought us *Das Goldene Vliess* which hangs in the Temple of the Muses. His name shines there—is is Franz Grillparzer.[2]

---

[2] Franz Grillparzer (1791–1872) was considered Austria's greatest dramatic poet. Although he was successful, he found himself in conflict with censors several times and was much embittered. In 1832 he was made Director of the Court Household Archives. There is a monument to him in the Volksgarten, and many other memories of him in Vienna today. Andersen first met him in Vienna in 1834.

Flight to the North

June 28, 1841

It will soon be spring. The birds are going north and so am I—but on wings of steam. For the steamship goes homewards from the royal capital of Bohemia. Well-known colorful pictures float by—summer-fair countryside, friendly faces; music sounds, the hours vanish and before I know it, I am in the North. . . .

The flag waves on the *Bohemia*[1] and like a fish in the water it shoots downstream between picturesque wooded hills. There is a flag on every ruin, and in every little town we fly past we are greeted with music; people wave their hats, small cannons salute and echo answers—it is a delightful journey!

We have on board a Copenhagener with his daughter. "It is very nice," she says, "but the water is disgustingly yellow." "Those are terrifying mountains," says the father, "just look at that fellow over there! I will not climb up there, one can see just as well down below."

But that one does not do! Go and climb the mountain, let the fresh mountain air blow around you and be grateful for the grandeur of nature abroad and for the good things at home.

Now Dresden lies before us in the heavy air—the Florence of Northern Germany. Dresden is a friend from whom one will not willingly part; it has something—what shall I call it—half bourgeois, half romantic; its garden is the mountain landscape, its study is the gallery with wonderful paintings. The new theater is a picture book, colorful and beautiful with gold and spirals. Inside one is overwhelmed by all the splendid decoration. Portraits of poets and writers decorate the ceiling; the boxes are gilded and airy.

---

[1] This is the first steamship to go between Prague and Dresden. It began its schedule about a month before my arrival. HCA.

July 3–5, 1841

It is good to be here, but we must hurry away . . . the steam engine roars away over meadow and field to Leipzig, to Magdeburg and with steam again to the outermost corner of Germany, mighty Hamburg. It is only a short flight, the hours can be counted—but we stop on the way, stop for some days. Melodies have an especial power, friendship and admiration are just as powerful—and Mendelssohn-Bartholdy lives in Leipzig.

It was so very pleasant and comfortable in his home, with his beautiful and friendly wife and everything done to honor the visitor. A little morning concert was given in Mendelssohn's drawing room. Frau von Goethe from Weimar and I were the fortunate guests. In church, on the same organ on which Johann Sebastian Bach played, Mendelssohn played one of Bach's fugues and a couple of his own lyrical pieces. Mountain and valley, heaven and hell poured forth their hymn through the organ pipes. . . .

July 6, 1841

The steam engine flies with the flight of the swallow. We are in Magdeburg. We shall sleep here tonight; we are again on the Elbe.

The boat is dirty and heavy. It suddenly stops in its tracks, then goes a little way, runs aground and then starts up again. The beauty of the landscape around is confined to a single poplar tree and a grassy field. It is cold and gray. The poet must come to the aid of nature just as nature has always aided him. The passengers on the ship are reading as in a library. What book is it in which two people at once are so engrossed?—it is a book by a Dane. Never say that Denmark has no mountains—its literature is a mountain, high and wooded, it can be seen from the neighboring countries, bluish on the horizon. We welcome you: come and stroll through our spiritual mountain country.

Soon our Elbe trip is finished; it is the last evening. How gray and cold it is! The swallows fly across the river to their holes in the banks, to their nests under the roof.

In the spring, the swallow comes from the warm lands, instinct drives it towards the North, leading it through the desert air to its nest. By the yellow rolling river with the poor green banks stands a little house with a flowering elderbush. "I must go there" cheeps the swallow, "it will take away my longing for the tall palm, the shady plane tree. The elderbush smells so sweet. On the doorstep sits the old grandmother in the warm sunshine, looking out at the ships. A little girl sits on her stool and makes merry over the flowered material in grandmamma's skirt!" Poor swallow—you come back, but the elderbush has been chopped down, grandmother is in her grave, the little girl is out in the world with strangers, and the new owner does not like swallows' nests. How everything has changed!

July 12, 1841, Hamburg

It is morning. Wrapped in a cold raw fog Hamburg's towers lie before us. We are in the North! The milk colored waves of the Elbe break against our ugly steamer. We land, we drive through the narrow dark streets. Here there is music and tonight a great musical festival will shine with light over the Alster and under the green avenues. Liszt is here—I shall hear him again, in the same hall as on my outward journey, hear again his *Valse Infernale*. One could really believe that my whole journey had been but a dream under Liszt's rushing fantasies. Not months, but only minutes have gone by.

"Time has taken a step forward," say my many fellow-countrymen. "While you have been away we have made much progress—we have got the omnibus in Copenhagen!" Yes, we go forward, I say myself as, during my walk, I see Heiberg's name on the corner of the Altona. A traveling Danish company is playing Heiberg vaudevilles. If his name gets as far as the Elbe it will easily fly over it—that will put him in good humor and will be good for him and for us too.

Music sounds, fireworks burst—Goodbye!—over the swelling sea to the green islands.

I have never known homesickness, unless it is homesickness for the heart to be filled with a wonderful love at the thought of the dear ones at home—an endless delight that colors the moment when one will first see them again in the familiar surroundings. This picture is so vivid that tears come into one's eyes, the heart is softened and one must make an effort to tear oneself away from these thoughts. If this is homesickness, then I do know it—and well. The first moment of one's return is the bouquet of the whole journey!

Index